THE KALAM EFFECT

P.M. NAIR was born on 18 October 1944 in Kerala. After completing his post-graduation in Economics at the University College, Thiruvananthapuram in 1966, he joined the Indian Administrative Service in 1967 and was allotted to the Union Territories Cadre, later known as the Arunachal Pradesh, Goa, Mizoram and Union Territories (AGMUT) Cadre. He has held the posts of Chief Secretary, Pondicherry and Arunachal Pradesh, among others. He was working as Secretary, Department of Defence Production & Supplies, Ministry of Defence in 2002 when A.P.J. Abdul Kalam selected him as his Secretary. Nair functioned as Secretary to the President for full five years, from July 2002 to July 2007.

# THE KALAM EFFECT

## MY YEARS WITH THE PRESIDENT

P.M. NAIR

*With 16 pages of colour photographs*

*Foreword by*

FALI S. NARIMAN

HarperCollins *Publishers* India

First published in hardback in 2008 by
HarperCollins *Publishers* India

First published in paperback in 2011

HarperCollins Publishers India, Cyber City, Building 10-A, Gurugram,
Haryana-122002, India
www.harpercollins.co.in

4 6 8 10 9 7 5 3

P-ISBN: 978-81-7223-930-5
E-ISBN: 978-93-5029-239-6



Typeset in 11/15 Minion Roman at
SURYA

Printed and bound at
MicroPrints India, New Delhi

MIX
Paper
FSC FSC™ C218906

This product is made of FSC®-certified and other controlled material.

HarperCollins Publishers, Macken House, 39/40 Mayor Street
Upper, Dublin 1, D01 C9W8, Ireland

# Contents

# Preface to the Paperback Edition

It is some years now since *The Kalam Effect: My Years with the President* was published in hardcover. It will reach an even wider audience now that it is coming out in paperback. It was a pleasure to serve with Dr A.P.J. Abdul Kalam when he was President. His presidency remains a noteworthy one for the initiatives, decisions and warmth he brought to the highest office in the land, examples of which abound in the book. Someday soon, I hope, he will write about the years in office from his perspective. He was probably the most travelled president ever. He would also hold the record for his engagement with people, whether in Rashtrapati Bhavan or outside it, meeting people of all ages and from all walks of life, and connecting with them. Notable, however, is how he has organized his routine post-presidency. After he demitted office as the President of India, Dr Kalam has been just as busy travelling as before. He is on tour for over 250 days in a year. Apart from addressing scientific communities across the globe, he continues to interact with children and students of all ages in schools and universities in India and abroad. He continues to be a rare icon, adored, loved and respected wherever he goes. As President or now, he remains a fantastic—his favourite word—role model to follow. Dear reader, it was an extremely enjoyable experience writing this book. I hope you will enjoy it just as much.

# Acknowledgements

I acknowledge my immeasurable gratitude to N. Venkatesan, my Private Secretary, who in spite of an extraordinarily busy schedule typed out my almost unreadable manuscript without mistakes, in good time. I must also thank Sowmya Srikanth, my Personal Assistant, who helped him in the task.

I cannot adequately thank R. Sunderaraj, a senior IPS officer who worked with me in Lakshadweep and Pondicherry, for the valuable advice given to me on various occasions all these five years, as well as for motivating me to write this book.

I must gratefully acknowledge the enormous help given to me by T.S. Ashok, Deputy Director (Photography) and Samar Mondol, Junior Photographer, who have provided the photographs that add such value to the text.

Ashok Kumar Mangotra, Joint Secretary to the President and Barun Mitra, Joint Secretary (Constitutional Affairs), who were two of the very senior members of my team, took the trouble of going through each word of the manuscript and gave me valuable advice. Allow me to express my sincere gratitude to both of them.

My wife Chandralekha, my sons Raajesh and Raakesh and my daughters-in-law Poonam and Divya were a continuous source of encouragement for me to write these memorable experiences.

Above all, I must wholeheartedly express my gratitude to Dr A.P.J. Abdul Kalam, who, when he became the President, chose me as his Secretary and enabled me to live those 'fantastic' five years the way I did from 2002 to 2007.

# Preface

I was Secretary to Dr A.P.J. Abdul Kalam when he was the President of India from 2002 to 2007. *The Kalam Effect* is my account of those extraordinary five years. It is by no means an attempt at a biography, nor a chronicle of Dr Kalam's scientific pursuits. As Secretary to the President, I was very close to him all these five years; yet I maintained a certain objectivity too. I saw his myriad facets. However, this is not an attempt at either defining or deifying him. It is only a narration of what I saw and experienced in that time. I have taken special care to see that there is not the slightest exaggeration in my recounting of the experience. I have very clearly called white white and black black and there has not been the slightest attempt to indulge in *suppressio veri, suggestio falsi*—suppressing the truth to suggest a falsehood.

Kalam has his strengths and weaknesses: he is a human being just like you and me. To which I might add, a good human being. Archbishop Tutu once said about Nelson Mandela, 'He was a good man, and did good things.' How true this is of Kalam too!

And here he is, for you, dear reader, to see him as I saw him.

# Foreword

No man is a hero to his secretary, but there are times when the secretary gets so infatuated with his master (the 'Boss') that he feels compelled to write a eulogy—as Boswell did of Samuel Johnson.

This book, however, is not a eulogy. It is a well-documented appreciation of P.M. Nair's days with President A.P.J. Abdul Kalam, recounted with frankness, sincerity and affectionate reverence, and without all the flattery and fawning. The book is therefore the easier to read; it is at once 'chatty' and personal without being impertinent. If I were asked to describe the contents of this book in just two words, I would unhesitatingly say: 'extremely readable'.

It is an account replete with fascinating colour pictures, but also shades of grey. President Kalam was not a politician but he was politically savvy—for instance on whether Afzal Khan should or should not hang he played his cards close to his chest, never revealing his hand. He would not tell those who met him what his decision would be when the government's recommendation came—although he had proclaimed on several occasions his abhorrence of the death penalty!

He was a good listener and an innovator in the art of communication. He daily visited (and was proud of) his own website answering questions posed to him by virtually all and sundry. No wonder that he was known and loved as the People's President. He faced—like all Presidents must—difficult decisions: the Bihar Dissolution Bill, the Office of Profit Bill and others, mentioned by the author in some detail, but with impeccable detachment. Nair's book is not a commissioned work prompted by Dr Kalam; on the contrary it contains the spontaneous impressions of a man who has worked under another, greater man, and enjoyed every minute of it!

President Kalam's creative and innovative emphasis on spiritual values was like a ray of sunlight in the lives of India's citizens. He is still a perennial source of inspiration to them—especially the young. He combined in one integrated personality a rare humanism with a background of distinguished scientific achievement.

He was also seemingly naïve, at times child-like—and yet, quite paradoxically, astute as well. In February 2005 I was witness to a bit of astute constitutional statesmanship by the country's President: when he delivered his customary address to both Houses of Parliament to herald in the new session. As you know India's Constitution provides that the

President is to address the Houses of Parliament at the beginning of each session. It does not say who is to prepare this address—this is decided by convention. The President acts only on the advice of his Council of Ministers, and this address is prepared by the government of the day. But on the morning of 25 February 2005 President Kalam made a departure—he had with him the full text of the written speech prepared by his government. But he chose to begin with a poem in Tamil, a poem composed not by the government of the day but by himself the previous night. He called it 'Where Are We'?

Where are we?
Where are we now, dear friends,
In the Maha Sabha that shapes as history,
The call of heartbeats of Indian people,
People ask us, people ask us:
Oh! Parliamentarians, the sculptors of Mother India,
Lead us unto light, enrich our lives.
Your righteous toil is our guiding light,
If you work hard, we all can prosper.
Like king, so the people,
Nurture great thoughts, rise up in actions,
May righteous methods be your guide;
May you all prosper ever with Almighty's grace.

It was a criticism of parliamentarians and their erstwhile manner of functioning—firmly expressed, but with a light touch. It was meant as a gentle exhortation from the people's President to the country's representatives not to walk out of legislative chambers, but to work hard and do their job. Since the President could not alter the text of his address to the Houses of Parliament, he devised the expedient of saying what he had to say in verse—and it was well received!

But no man is without blemish and if a recorder is to be truthful he must paint his subject as Oliver Cromwell commanded the great portrait painter of his time, Sir Peter Lely, to do, when he sat for his picture—

> . . . use all your skill to paint my picture truly like me, and not flatter me at all: but remark all these *roughnesses, pimples, warts* and everything as you see in me, otherwise I will never pay a farthing for it!

There are no 'roughnesses' in these pages because Dr Kalam is by nature kind and compassionate. But there are some 'pimples' and 'warts'—which give a holistic picture of the man who was our President for one full term, and in my opinion (and in the opinion of many) richly deserved another.

In this book there are also 'revelations' unknown to many, one of which I found particularly significant. Let me quote Mr Nair:

> Once he called the former Chief Justice of India, Mr Justice Venkatachaliah, from Bangalore for some consultation. They were together in the Study for a

> few minutes, sitting side by side on the same sofa. I was called in at the end of this meeting and I went with Justice Venkatachaliah to his room. We sat in silence for quite a while, and then he said 'Mr Nair, this was an experience of a lifetime. I was sitting so close to Dr Kalam and I could feel palpable sensations of godliness and divinity reverberating in me. I was nervous. He is really God's own man.

A fine tribute to a great man, by another!

**Fali S. Nariman**

# THE KALAM EFFECT

# 1

'I want to meet you urgently, alone.' It was Dr A.S. Pillai, Distinguished Scientist from DRDO, on the telephone. It was 10.30 a.m. on 18 July 2002. I was to leave late in the afternoon for Bangalore to visit HAL (Hindustan Aeronautics Ltd) and I had to prepare for that.

'Could you come right away?' I asked Pillai.

'In fifteen minutes,' he said, and rang off.

What could it be? Pillai sounded excited. I sat clueless. It was only eighteen days since I had taken charge as Secretary, Defence Production, moving from the MNES (Ministry of Non-Conventional Energy Sources) to my old haunt, where I had served as Joint Secretary for four years. I was starting to thoroughly enjoy my second stint there and looking forward to meeting my old friends in the PSUs and ordnance factories and renewing our association.

The knock on the door was followed by a hurried entry

by Pillai, who was out of breath from having trudged up the stairs. He took a seat, looked around to ensure that we had privacy and then leaned forward. 'I am coming from Kalam. He wants you,' he said. I was listening, but it didn't register.

'Say it again,' I said.

'Dr Kalam wanted me to tell you that he wants you,' Pillai repeated. 'As his Secretary. Secretary to the President.'

Kalam had just been elected the 12th President of India. The results were declared on 17 July. He had won hands down in a contest whose result was a foregone conclusion. But what Pillai told me was not even in my distant thoughts. I sat back, unable to react. Then the words came.

'I am sorry; I don't know. I am happy, very happy where I am . . .' I muttered.

Now the look of disbelief was on Pillai's face. I gathered myself and wanted to explain, but before I could, Pillai ventured, 'Kalam knows that you are going to be Cabinet Secretary one day, but he says that he will ensure that you will not lose that chance.' The chances of my becoming Cabinet Secretary were slim, but I didn't say so.

'No, no, no, Dr Pillai. I can give you a list of some excellent officers who will be a great help to Dr Kalam,' I offered. I took out the Civil List from the side table and patiently explained to him how P.V. Rajaraman of Tamil Nadu cadre, K.R. Nair of Punjab cadre and B.S. Baswan of M.P. cadre would be ideally suited for this job. They were all my batchmates (IAS 1967), people whom I had always held in very high esteem for sheer efficiency, integrity and honesty.

Pillai, apparently fed up, rose and left saying that he would convey this to Kalam.

I looked at the closed door, fumbled for the non-existent cigarette and scratched my head, feeling helpless and miserable in my uncertainty. Did I do right? Wasn't I being foolish? But then, I was really happy in my present job. Why should I move? I had to do something. I must ask for a second opinion. I must seek advice, but from whom?

I looked at the clock. It was approaching noon. I reached for the RAX. The Cabinet Secretary, T.R. Prasad. I rang him up. Luckily, he was not in a meeting. 'Sir, I want to meet you very urgently. Something personal. Only two minutes.' I didn't wait for a reply from Prasad. I rushed out and drove straight to Rashtrapati Bhavan—to the Cabinet Secretary's office, of course.

Mercifully, Prasad was free. A little breathlessly but with some pride, I repeated to him my conversation with Pillai a few minutes ago. Hadn't I done well, I thought to myself, and eagerly awaited a pat from the Cabinet Secretary. 'Don't be a stupid fool,' he said. 'It's an honour to be the Secretary to the President. You're lucky he wants you. Say yes without losing time. Use this phone.' I stared at him, realized he was right and rushed back to South Block.

Luckily, Pillai was available on the telephone. He hadn't yet conveyed anything to Kalam. 'Please tell him I am ready to be his Secretary. I feel honoured,' I finished.

I wanted to tell somebody. Chandralekha, my wife would

still be at school. I could speak to my elder son. So I rang up Raajesh in London and conveyed the news. 'Achan (dad), why do you want to take it up? Aren't you happy in Defence Production?' He sounded quite sure. This made me thoughtful again. I sank back in my chair.

I dialled Pillai again. He hadn't told Kalam anything. 'Please tell him to give me four days to decide. Let me come back from Bangalore.' Pillai agreed, his resentment at my vacillation hardly hidden.

Files could wait. Lunch could wait. Something had to be done. I had to decide where I wanted to be once and for all. And I needed help.

P.G. Muralidharan was nine years senior to me in the IAS. An officer of integrity, with clarity of thought and excellent judgment. He had retired from service and had come to Delhi from Kerala to be with his son. I had known him since 1964. I dialled his number.

'Don't be a b . . . y fool,' he said, the second time in less than one hour I had been told this by two different persons whose judgment I could never question. 'Accept it straightaway. Don't ask for four days to decide. Today, right now.' He was matter of fact. A no-nonsense man, as always. Pillai again. I had decided, at last. He would convey my yes to Kalam in the evening.

As I flew to Bangalore in the evening, considering how the day's events had come about, I thought back to my first interaction with Kalam twenty-one years ago, at the Vikram Sarabhai Space Centre, Thumba.

# 2

I was at Kavaratti. I was posted (normally referred to as shunted) as Administrator of Lakshadweep in 1978. The islands were nice to me and my family and I thoroughly enjoyed our stay there. I was fortunate to receive two of India's Prime Ministers there in the space of two years—Morarji Desai and Indira Gandhi.

I was in the third year of my stay there. 1981. There was a call from Bangalore, from none other than the redoubtable Seshan—T.N. Seshan, then Joint Secretary, Department of Space, who later made such a mark as the Chief Election Commissioner of India. He wanted me as Controller, Vikram Sarabhai Space Centre, Thumba. And when Seshan from Space said anything, it was an order. I said 'Yes.' Time, tide and even space didn't wait for him and nor did he for any of them. I knew that only too well then; the country knew it later.

I joined VSSC as Controller in June 1981. I was being exposed to an utterly new experience—that of mingling with the scientific community. It was fascinating in many ways, frustrating in some. Bureaucrats were certainly not the toast of the Centre. They were just tolerated, as a necessary evil. Supercilious smiles and condescending looks greeted me everywhere. But there was one silver lining, a notable exception—Dr S. Ramnath.

Ramnath was officiating as Controller, and I was to take charge from him. Little did I know then that he was the younger brother of Subramaniam Chandrasekhar, the famous astrophysicist who would win the Nobel Prize for Physics in 1983. Ramnath was a good person, extraordinarily so—the first true scientist I met who impressed me first with his humility, then with his professional ability.

I had been a student of economics. I knew nothing of science. I used to joke with my colleagues in the Space Centre that all that I knew about missiles and rocketry was their spelling and not their science. As a bureaucrat, I was supposed to know administration. I did not know if I did, but I told them I did.

It was there that I met Kalam. A senior scientist, and a bachelor. I met him first at the Friday meeting of the Director, where all the senior scientists and the Controller discussed matters scientific and otherwise and arrived at no decision. Dr S.C. Gupta, M.R. Kurup, R. Aravamudan were all there, apart from Kalam. Dr V.R. Gowariker, Director of the Centre, would preside over the meetings. Kalam stood out in the group—for his gentlemanliness, pleasant disposition and sheer cheer. The scientific insights were totally lost on me. I liked him for what I saw in him. I hadn't gauged the depths yet.

I cannot claim that I moved very closely with Kalam during my VSSC days. I bumped into him quite a few times, to be greeted by a hello and a smile that were both warmer and lasted longer than that of most people. I came to know him as a bachelor scientist wedded only to his scientific pursuits, a person who did not know the difference between day and night. His working day very often extended far into the night—or rather, early morning—and often the day would start again long before the sun rose. He was the darling of the 4,000-strong workforce who carried him on their shoulders when India's satellite launch vehicle SLV-3 was first put into orbit and then when he was awarded the Padma Bhushan. I knew too that his peers, not all of them but certainly many of them, did not fall into that category: I knew that some of them had distributed sweets when SLV-3 in its first flight plunged into the sea. For decency's sake, I shall not dwell upon it any further.

✦

The airhostess announced we would shortly be landing at Bangalore. I put aside my thoughts and got ready to step out.

# 3

22 July 2002. I had just returned to Delhi. I half-expected an enthusiastic group of my friends to greet me at the airport. After all, I was going to be Secretary to the President of India. But of course, no one was there. The Protocol Officer of the MNES received me as usual. Where was all the excitement? I was getting panicky. Did Kalam have second thoughts?

I rushed home and went on the Net. Whispersinthecorridors.com. No. Not even a murmur there! My heart sank. I went to South Block and dialled Pillai.

Pillai perked up my spirits. Kalam wanted me to meet him. That evening. Perhaps a little later. Pillai would check and let me know.

8.30 p.m. that day saw me and Pillai at Asiad Village in south Delhi, so called because it was built to house the 1982 Asian Games athletes. It was quite a job to pass through the security cordon and gain access to Kalam's small, functional flat. We were finally able to reach the anteroom. We waited, as did many others there and outside.

There was a flurry of activity and then Kalam, the President-to-be, came in. He gestured to H. Sheridon and R.K. Prasad, his secretaries, and Pillai that he wanted to talk to me alone. And then we were together, only the two of us. He was most unlike a President-to-be. Calm and modest as usual, despite the deluge of attention and the intense media focus, wearing his unmistakable blue shirt and smiling in his disarming way. It was 'fantastic'.

I spent twenty minutes with him. He reminded me of our days at the VSSC. I felt specially touched when he recalled the 'train episode'. When I was in Thumba, the drivers of the 100-odd buses of the centre suddenly went on a strike, almost paralysing work there as the VSSC was located over twenty kilometres from the city. I was fortunate, with the immediate and generous help of T.N. Seshan and K. Neelakantan, a cousin who was a very senior officer in Southern Railway at that time, to be able to run a special train from Trivandrum Central to Veli, near the VSSC, for almost a month and a half, which finally broke the strike and the centre returned to normal. Kalam must have been extremely happy that work could go on in the normal way once more. His smile when he met me after the strike was over conveyed that eloquently. R.B. Sreekumar, an IPS officer of Gujarat cadre who was the Commandant of the

Central Industrial Security Force guarding the space centre, was a tremendous source of strength to me in the entire operation. Sreekumar made a name for himself in course of time setting standards of high integrity, honesty and efficiency in the police service. Kalam was referring to the strike and my handling of it. That seemed to be the turning point for me. He wanted me as his Secretary. I asked him if I could say so in as many as words to the Cabinet Secretary. He said yes.

✦

The next morning saw me again at the Cabinet Secretariat. T.R. Prasad rang up the President-to-be and got his reconfirmation of what I had conveyed. Yes, the orders would be issued in a day or two.

It was final. I called on the RM (Raksha Mantri—Defence Minister) George Fernandes and told him about it. He wished me well, as he had always done. I told my colleagues, friends and relatives. I started looking forward to my new innings.

The order was issued on 24 July.

# 4

25 July 2002. The 12th President of India was to be sworn in in the solemn and historic Central Hall of Parliament. I hadn't got a pass to attend the function, but I somehow managed to get one and got in.

It was a grand function. For the first time, hundreds of children had been brought in as special invitees. Justice B.N. Kirpal, the Chief Justice of India, administered the oath. The speech that Kalam delivered after being sworn in was not a mere formality: he spoke eloquently, from the heart, as he set out his agenda for the nation. That of a Developed Nation—India Vision 2020. And to underline the urgency of the task before the nation, he invoked Kabir, 'Kal kare so aaj kar, Aaj kare so ab (What you will do tomorrow do today, what you will do today, do it now).'

The ceremonial formalities followed—the Guard of Honour, the send-off to the outgoing President, K.R.

Narayanan. Kalam had been asked if he wanted to be sworn in at any special time that he considered auspicious. His answer was that any time was auspicious.

Twenty minutes after Kalam became President of India, I took charge as his Secretary. Shamsher Sheriff ushered me into my office, a long elegant room at the northern end of Rashtrapati Bhavan, which had been lying untenanted for over two years. After Gopalkrishna Gandhi left in 2000, there was no Secretary; Shamsher Sheriff, Joint Secretary, managed everything.

At 3 p.m., I was called to the Study, as the room in which the President sits is called. Barun Mitra, Director (Constitutional Affairs), an IAS officer of 1987 batch, had given me a few papers which included a letter from a Governor who wanted permission to come to Delhi for a few days on medical grounds. I mentioned this to the President as he sat at his desk at one end of the Study, near the french windows overlooking the Mughal Gardens, where a fountain sprayed water quietly. He looked up and said, 'Yes, I can well understand that some of them would like to be in Delhi—obviously for medical reasons! Okay, I agree.' Sheridon, Prasad and I looked at one another in silence that spoke volumes.

The President had arrived.

# 5

The next day, his first full day in office. I was called to the Study. There I saw Kalam, sans the blue shirt but with the same infectious grin and the hair, long and curling over his forehead, well in place. I took my seat and he started. 'Mr Nair (for some reason that is still not known to me but only to him, Kalam always called me Mr Nair!), we have five years. I have a mission and we shall achieve it. I need your assistance and support.'

I said, 'Sir, you have chosen me as your Secretary against all kinds of advice given to you and from among all the names suggested to you. I feel honoured, but sir, if you want me to deliver, allow me to choose my own team.'

'Fantastic,' he said. 'Go ahead.'

And select the team, I did. Right from the Joint Secretary to the President, the Military Secretary and other officers including the ADCs. All were selected by me after interviewing them along with the others who had been called. Kalam did not interfere at all; that was the trust he reposed in me. Events in the course of the five years that flew by vindicated this trust. The team delivered. My letter to the members of my team that I wrote on the eve of Kalam's demitting office, included at the end of this book, says it all.

# 6

'Sir, the morning meeting today will be in the afternoon,' Venkatesan, my Senior PS, announced. Bemused, I asked him when. 'Sheridon says it will be around 3.30.' I hoped it was not 3.30 a.m., although that, being morning, would have been appropriate for a morning meeting. I thanked my stars, as for Kalam a full working day included the night. Sheridon was one of his senior Private Secretaries, and a man of unusual competence and loyalty who stood steadfast with Kalam along with Prasad, the other senior Private Secretary who had the same qualities in equal measure. I waited for the clock to strike 3.30.

'Sir, the morning meeting will now be held at 3.45,' Usha Sudhindra, my other Private Secretary, informed me at about 3 p.m. By then I had realized such delays and postponements were going to be part of my life, and wasn't surprised.

'Morning meetings' were held to discuss the various papers, petitions and applications received by the President as also the files sent to him for approval or final decision. Kalam's mornings started like they do for all of us, but his 'fantastic' communing with birds, animals and other creatures housed in the bio-diversity park that he developed kept him busy with Mother Nature during his morning walks, which were followed by his meticulous scrutiny of the newspapers and then, of course, the Web. Thus breakfast would be around noon and then office, beginning with the 'morning meeting' in the afternoon.

Any paper that was sent to him, any file that was put up to him would come up for discussion in the morning meeting. The Military Secretary and I were fixtures in these meetings. The former would brief him on the ceremonies slated for the day, the dos and don'ts and the 'musts', and after he left I would discuss the papers and files with him. As the months passed I used to induct my senior colleagues like Ashok Mangotra, the Joint Secretary, and Barun Mitra and Satish Mathur, the Directors, to help me tide over the mornings without hiccups!

For Kalam, nothing was unimportant—everything, every scrap of paper needed to be gone into and studied. And one couldn't fool him by ignoring any papers. His memory was amazing—photographic, and with plenty of film to register information.

The following instance is one of many examples. The

President was away on tour for about two days and the letters and petitions had piled up. On an average he used to get 70 to 100 petitions a day—all marked to me for MM (morning meeting). The ones that were received before he left on tour had been already marked for MM and those that were received during his absence were seen by him during his 'lunch' at around 10 p.m., after his return, and then marked to me. If breakfast was at noon, lunch could naturally be far behind, with dinner spilling over to the early hours of the next day!

So the papers all came. I went through each one of them and as usual made cryptic notes on them on Post-its so that I could advise him intelligently on each. There was a petition from the students of ITI, Thanjavur. I explained to the President the contents of the petition and said I would forward it to the Collector, Thanjavur and ask for a report on what he could do to solve their problems. Kalam listened to me and said, 'There is one more representation.'

I said, 'No, sir, that is only a copy.' He: 'No, there is another.' I: 'It's a copy.' He repeated, 'No, Mr Nair, there is another representation.' And I, with whom all the papers were for the past three days, and was as usual confident of my capacity to remember things, said almost with finality, 'No, sir. You were away on tour. I have gone through each of these papers. What you are referring to is perhaps a copy of this petition.' The President said, 'Okay. Let's discuss the others.'

We did, and then the files, and I returned to my room. I was rather uneasy because Kalam had said five times that there was another representation and six times I had said no. I decided to go through all the papers once again. And I froze. There *was* another representation from another section of the students of ITI, Thanjavur! I felt ashamed and inadequate. I rushed down to the Study and said, 'Sir, I apologize. There *was* another representation. You were right. I was wrong. I somehow missed it. I am sorry, sir, it will not happen again.' Kalam simply smiled and said, 'Okay, don't worry. I know you will take action on that representation also.' I retreated, feeling humbled.

Kalam's capacity to remember things was 'fantastic', to use his own pet expression. He used to get numerous books for review and mercifully instead of me, he would pass them on to Mangotra. Mangotra would spend sleepless nights preparing notes so that he could discuss them with the President in the next morning meeting. As a permanent adjunct, I would be present then too. Mangotra would explain what the book was all about, how good or bad it was, etc. Suddenly, the President would say, 'Mangotraji, did you see para 2 on page 24? What a beautiful thought! Please convey my greetings (to the author) for the good thoughts.' I would take the book from Mangotra, turn to page 24, para 2 and there it would be—a really beautiful passage! This happened on several occasions.

And the bureaucrat that I was, having been bred and

nurtured to observe everything with suspicion in officialdom, where everyone is dishonest unless shown to be otherwise or has been certified as honest by a politician, decided to test Kalam. When another book was reviewed, he wanted us to see page 96 and said that apparently what the author stated was substantially true. Then I said, 'Sir, do you really think he meant it when he said what he did on page 96?'

'No, Mr Nair, he has contradicted himself on page 154, where he says just the opposite of what he had said on page 96,' came the reply!

# 7

A.P.J. Abdul Kalam is a man just like anyone of us—well, perhaps, not quite. Quite a few shades better, but, during those five years I was with him, I noticed a few of his flaws and foibles too.

Kalam was never known for his punctuality. I used to wonder if he had a watch at all. He had, perhaps one too many. That must have been the reason. The morning meetings scheduled at 2.30 p.m. never started at 2.30 p.m. Always 20 to 30 minutes late. His departure timings on tours in India and even abroad had gone for sixes—I knew he was a cricket fan, but this was a different game!

As his Secretary, I could never justify these delays. And I am sure he won't mind my saying so, because he always faces up to the truth.

His lack of punctuality had come in for a lot of criticism. Normally, whenever the President went on tour inside India or outside, police deployment would be done well in advance. Almost three hours before his departure or arrival, the policemen would be detailed on duty along the route. And they would go home only two or three hours after the President had left or arrived. None would mind this much in the normal course. But in winter? The President is scheduled to leave at 8 p.m. The police constables are on duty from 5 p.m. The President starts at 8.30 p.m. The policemen remain on duty. He leaves. The policemen all along the route are picked up after 9.30 p.m. and taken to the respective police stations and from there they go home on their own and some are staying quiet far off, in outlying areas. They reach home early morning for having done their duty from 5 p.m. Sad! Perhaps Kalam didn't know the gravity of this. I told him about it and I know his heart bled. The next two to three programmes went on schedule. Then again, the old routine.

We have heard that many scientists are eccentric. As if, most of us, non-scientists, are not! Kalam was a scientist, but also a President, and on this score, I hold no brief for him. Even as a scientist President, he should have known that by sticking to his timings as scheduled, he was respecting others' time as they too had their lives to live and their personal obligations to fulfil.

Here Kalam failed, not knowingly, not wilfully, but in spite of himself.

I remembered what Chellamma teacher had told me

when I was in 3rd class. 'To err is human.' I didn't know what it meant at that time, of course. But it does help accept others' failings, I suppose.

# 8

Kalam's moving into Rashtrapati Bhavan had its sidelights. More so, perhaps, because he was a bachelor!

I received a letter from a lady (whose name I will not reveal) in Patna which read as follows:

> Subject: I offer myself for the post of official Hostess (1st Lady) of Rashtrapati Bhawan.
>
> Most Respected Sir,
>
> I am ready to offer myself as an official Hostess of Rashtrapati Bhawan. I am fifty years of age with pleasing personality.
>
> I have done my Master's Degree from Patna University.
>
> My favourite subject is Home Science. I believe in Hospitality i.e. welcome and kindness to visitors in much better way.

> Herewith I am sending my photograph for your kind perusal. I have taken consent of my husband Prof.—, who is a free minded social being. He always wants to give help the person in need. We are only two persons in the house.
>
> Therefore, please give me a chance to serve you all and oblige.

I did not know what she meant by saying that her husband was a 'free minded social being'.

Kalam didn't need a First Lady. He was a superb host in his own inimitable way. Hundreds of banquets and social gatherings went by without anyone feeling the absence of a First Lady. Kalam was all that mattered.

# 9

14 August 2003. We are in the middle of the monsoon, but what a bright and sunny day! The sun at its sparkling best. And my heart doing an extra beat, as I am happy to see the clear skies. The next day the President hosts a reception for dignitaries and people from all walks of life. The President would be 'at home' to them in the central lawns of Rashtrapati Bhavan. If the number of people who came to greet him on New Year's Day that year was any indication, a crowd of three to four thousand could be expected on Independence Day. And the central lawns could accommodate them comfortably. I went to sleep and thought later that I had slept well.

On the 15th, I thought it was 6.30 a.m. when I woke up, but the clock showed it was 8.25 a.m. already. It was dark outside, and there was pouring rain, the dark clouds rolling in portending still heavier showers. I looked out and my heart sank. I knew I had to act but didn't know what I could do.

I went to office, called all my colleagues and by 10.20 a.m., I was in my room with all my senior colleagues. I looked out of the window, and they all did so too. And all our faces reflected our disappointment at what nature was perpetrating outside. And still more rain to come.

I asked my colleagues what we should do. The President's reception would start at 5.30 p.m. We couldn't hold it indoors because the guests would number in the thousands. I told Satish Mathur to arrange 2,000 umbrellas from somewhere. An efficient officer, he immediately contacted the army and the police and came back in twenty minutes and said, 'Sir, done.'

The President was in his bedroom upstairs. I wanted to meet him. I sent word. He said I could meet him at 12.10. As I entered his room, he said, 'O, Mr Nair look at that. What a wonderful day! It's so cool.' I was not feeling cool at all. I said, 'Sir, today you are hosting a reception for a few thousand people. What do we do in this weather?'

'Oh no, don't worry, we will have it inside,' he said.

'No, sir,' I said irritatedly. 'We can cater to a maximum of 600 to 700 people inside, not the two to three thousand that we are expecting. Of course, we have arranged two thousand umbrellas, but that may not be enough.'

The President looked at me and then at the ceiling and said resignedly, 'Okay, then what can we do? If it rains, we will get wet. That's all.'

Which did not comfort me much. I knew that if it rained, we would get wet. I was leaving his room in a mood no better than the one in which I had gone in. As I reached the end of the longish room on my way out, Kalam called. 'Mr Nair, come, why is your face like this?' I thought I had a good face, although my wife who had wholeheartedly supported that view initially had now begun to question it in subtle ways. But I could imagine I was not looking my best right now.

I stood still and asked, 'Sir, what?'

He said, 'Mr Nair, don't worry.' He pointed a hand skywards and continued, 'I have spoken there. Don't worry.'

I returned, mulling over the remark and wondering what he had said to whom in the skies. It was 12.38 p.m. then.

What happened then did seem a miracle, though. Around 2 p.m. the rain stopped. The sun came out and shone brilliantly; my team set about doing the arrangements for the reception in the lawns. The minutes ticked by and the sun was at its best.

5.30 p.m. The President arrived in procession, took the salute, mingled with the guests, chatted with them and had himself photographed with almost all of them. The guests had their tea and snacks and those who were lucky spoke with the President.

6.15 p.m. The conclusion of the ceremony. The President stood to attention; the National Anthem was played and he left in ceremonial procession preceded by two ADCs and followed by the Military Secretary and the Deputy Military Secretary. He reached the building and then—it started raining again! But the reception had gone off well.

*The Week* (31 August 2003) reported the event thus and I quote:

> **Thoughtful Nature**
>
> Mother Nature seems to have a reverential attitude to India's Independence Day. History records that a rainbow appeared as soon as the tricolour was hoisted at India Gate on the afternoon of August 15, 1947.
>
> President A.P.J. Abdul Kalam's at-home this year, too, was deferentially spared by monsoon clouds. It was pouring since the morning of the 15th, but the rain stopped an hour before the President was to arrive at the Mughal Gardens. And the moment he exited, it started drizzling, leaving the departing guests a little wet.
>
> All the same, the presidential staff was not quite willing to leave it to nature's goodwill. They had hired hundreds of umbrellas, just in case.

Incidentally, regarding those umbrellas, after the distinguished invitees had left, quite a few of them were found missing!

# 10

I am a firm believer in God, but I am not one of those who believe in godmen who claim to have extraordinary powers. But some things do defy normal logic and leave you dumbfounded and the usual response is 'these things happen'. As if that explains anything!

Kalam was undoubtedly the country's most mobile President ever. More than 175 tours—one almost every second week. Except for Lakshadweep, he had visited all the states and Union Territories by the end of his term. Visited is perhaps the wrong word for the kind of schedule he followed. He had toured rural areas and inspected development works going on everywhere. He wanted to visit Lakshadweep too in July 2007, but the heavy monsoon prevented the authorities from programming this tour.

In May 2003, President Kalam wanted to tour Orissa. His plan was to go to Bhubaneswar by fixed-wing aircraft and then go to Baripada, Rourkela, Chandikhol and Nirakarapur by helicopter. The dates were fixed for 14 and 15 May 2003.

12 May 2003. The morning meeting started, as usual, in the afternoon. Maj. Gen. K.S. Dogra, the Military Secretary, and I were with Kalam.

'Sir,' Dogra said, 'You are planning to go to Orissa on 14th, but I have reports that there is a cyclone moving towards Orissa from the Andhra coast.'

Kalam looked at him and then me and said, 'Let's see. We have two more days.' And then the morning meeting moved on, as usual, discussing relevant and irrelevant papers and files with equal gusto.

13 May 2003. Reports appeared in the Press that the cyclone was getting stronger and moving towards Orissa. The morning meeting again. Dogra was a worried man and rightly so.

'Sir, I think we have to call off this visit because this cyclone is to hit Orissa tomorrow.'

I looked at Kalam. There was great disappointment on his face. He lifted the telephone receiver and dialled the Met chief himself. 'Sir, there is no question of your going to Orissa because the cyclonic storm is hitting it tomorrow morning,' the Met chief told him. The forecast was clear enough. The President hung up. Pensive for a moment, he turned to Dogra and said, 'Let's ask the Air Force.'

Duly connected to the Ops Wing, the President himself spoke. 'Sir, we can take you to Bhubaneswar by fixed-wing aircraft, but your trip to the other places by helicopter is just not possible because of the cyclonic storm,' said the Air Marshal he spoke with. We could hear all this because the instrument was in speaker mode. Kalam put down the receiver and looked at us unhappily.

I paused for a moment and said, 'Sir, the Chief Secretary of Orissa is my batchmate. Let me speak to him and I'll come back to you around 3 p.m.' It was around 1 o'clock then. He agreed.

Dogra and I went to my room. I rang up Pratip Mohanty, my batchmate. 'How is the situation? What is it like? I am referring to the cyclone,' I said.

'Okay, PM (my friends always call me by my initials), it's very calm now, but the cyclone is, according to the Met Department, to hit Bhubaneswar tomorrow morning. We are ready with all arrangements for rescue operations,' replied Pratip.

Dogra was looking at me; I was looking at him too, but my mind was elsewhere. I said, 'General Saab, you heard what the CS said. The cyclone is hitting there tomorrow morning. Let's go to the President.'

We did. Kalam was looking rather distraught. I don't know what came over me. I said, 'Sir, you go to Orissa, as planned.'

I could feel Dogra's shock. Before the President could react, Dogra asked me, 'Sir, what are you saying? Cyclone is hitting there tomorrow and you are asking him to go?' I said, 'Yes. If it is bad, he will not go by helicopter to those villages, but he can certainly go to Bhubaneswar by the fixed-wing aircraft and complete the programmes there and come back. The President will go to Orissa as scheduled.' Dogra looked stunned. But Kalam was beaming, such assurance, however illogical, having been given by his Secretary.

What happened thereafter may be hard to believe. The Rashtrapati Bhavan tour section was readying itself for the Orissa tour starting the next morning. Dogra was packing his things for the tour much against his will. And then . . .

The Doordarshan news announced that the cyclone that was advancing menacingly towards Orissa was standing still and weakening too. The morning broke, Kalam went to Bhubaneswar, toured all the areas planned by helicopter and returned to Delhi.

The cyclone had receded.

The following reports of the Meteorological Department and those in the *Hindu* speak for themselves:

INDIA METEOROLOGICAL DEPARTMENT

No.BOB/06/2003 Dated May 14, 2003

Sub: Very Severe Cyclonic Storm over the Bay of Bengal

Ref: IMD note of even No. dated May 13, 2003

The Very Severe Cyclonic Storm over central Bay of Bengal has moved slowly northwards since yesterday. It is now centred 500 km south-east of Visakhapatnam. In view of this, south Andhra

Pradesh coast is de-alerted. However, the Cyclone Alert for north Andhra Pradesh and Orissa coasts continues.

Heavy to very heavy rainfall, accompanied with gale force winds associated with the system, is likely to commence over north Andhra Pradesh–Orissa coasts by tomorrow morning.

An update will be issued tomorrow.

(R.R. KELKAR)
Director General of Meteorology

The *Hindu*, dated Wednesday, 14 May 2003

**Cyclone Threat to A.P., Orissa**

By Our Staff Reporter

BHUBANESWAR, MAY 13: The severe cyclonic storm in the Bay of Bengal moved northwest and lay as a 'very severe cyclonic storm' about 900 km south-southwest of Paradip at 2.30 p.m. today.

The system is likely to intensify further in the north-northwesterly direction towards the northern Andhra Pradesh–Orissa coast, the Bhubaneswar Meteorological Centre said this evening.

Heavy to very heavy rain and strong winds associated are likely to commence over the coastal districts of Orissa during the next 48 hours. Fishermen have been advised not to venture into the sea.

*Our Hyderabad Special Correspondent writes:*

The storm that left Tamil Nadu side lay centred about 600 km southeast off Machilipatnam. The Meteorological Office here said that all 10 coastal districts had come under threat and that heavy rain, accompanied by gales with speed up to 200 kmph, were likely tomorrow.

The *Hindu*, dated Thursday, May 15, 2003

**Cyclone Weakens**

By Our Staff Reporter

BHUBANESWAR, MAY 14: The severe cyclonic storm over west central Bay has weakened and lay centred about 600 km south south-west of Paradip.

The cyclone was likely to move in a northerly direction towards north Andhra Pradesh and Orissa coast. Heavy rain is likely to occur along with strong wind over coastal Orissa by tomorrow morning, the Meteorological department said.

The *Hindu*, dated Friday, May 16, 2003

**Heavy Rain Forecast**

By Our Staff Reporter

BHUBANESWAR, MAY 15: The severe cyclonic storm over the west central Bay has remained stationary and lay centred about 600 km south southwest of Paradip, the weatherman at the Meteorological Centre here said this evening.

The system is likely to intensify further and move in a northerly direction towards north Andhra Pradesh and the Orissa coast. Heavy rain, coupled with strong winds, is likely to commence over all the 11 coastal districts from tomorrow morning.

The *Hindu*, dated Saturday, May 17, 2003

**Cyclone Threat Recedes**

By Our Staff Reporter

BHUBANESWAR, MAY 16: The cyclone threat over north Andhra Pradesh and Orissa coast was gone with the cyclonic storm over west central Bay losing strength and changing direction today. The storm remained stationary and lay centred about 550 km south of Paradip, according to the local weather office. It was likely to move in a northeasterly direction.

✦

There were other such instances. I shall mention only one more.

July 2005. The President's tour down south included visits to Thiruvananthapuram, Kochi and Alappuzha. On 29

July he was to go by helicopter from Kochi to Alappuzha. As we reached Nedumbassery airport at Kochi, the skies came down and the blinding downpour virtually flooded the environs. The pilot of the helicopter came over to meet the President and informed him that visibility was practically nil and that it was impossible to take off for Alappuzha. Kalam, cool as ever, told the Air Force Officer, 'Okay, we shall wait for half an hour and then see.'

Half an hour went by. A few minutes more. There was a slight let-up in the rains. The visibility was improving. The pilot was summoned and Kalam said, 'Let's go.'

The pilot was uncomfortable. Mustering courage, he respectfully muttered, 'Sir, no sir, the visibility at Alappuzha is practically zero and the indications are that it will continue to be so for quite some time more. We won't be able to land there, sir.'

Kalam looked around, then up, skywards, then down and asked, 'Can we take off from here?'

'Yes, sir, we can, but we can't land at Alappuzha,' the pilot said.

'Okay, we shall take off. If we can't land at Alappuzha, we can come back,' Kalam said with an air of finality. I was beside him. With a meaningful smile, he turned and whispered to me, 'We shall land too.'

We took off. Alappuzha was only about fifteen minutes away by helicopter. With visibility near zero there when we were airborne, we were sure that we would be back at Kochi in the next few minutes.

Ten minutes into the flight, however, the skies started clearing. We were above Alappuzha. Looking out through the window, I could see the helipads very clearly. The rain had stopped; the sun was out, shining bright. The entire city could be seen down below. The helicopter landed as smoothly and surely as ever. The rotor stopped; the door opened. Kalam, who was occupying the front seat, stood up, turned and looked at all of us who were seated behind, smiled, did a thumbs-up and alighted. We followed him, thoroughly mystified by the turn of events, but delighted all the same.

Kalam went through with all the programmes at Alappuzha as scheduled and returned to Kochi. Once again the weather gods had unbent. It could only be the innate goodness of the man that could be the reason for whatever had happened, we marvelled.

Shakespeare, as usual, put it nicely when he said, 'There are more things in heaven and earth, Horatio, than are dreamt of in your philosophy.'

# 11

Nothing was unimportant to Kalam, hence everything was important. We had received letters from people whose sanity was questionable, and even those letters were 'considered' and discussed. I recall a letter from one who described himself in print on his letterhead as 'World Leader' and 'President of the Globe', writing to Kalam as to what he should do to save the United States from Russia (which he referred to as USSR) through the Vatican and Mecca. And he signed it as 'Ambassador of God'. Even this letter came up for discussion in the morning meeting.

I had no option but to take the letter for discussion in the meeting. I said, 'Sir, some mad fellow has written this non-sense. Why should we waste our time?' Kalam said, 'Okay, if you say so, we won't take any action on it.'

I think it was in the first few weeks after he became President. An e-mail came from a young girl in Agra. It said,

'Uncle, in our area, there is only one park and in that park, there is only one see-saw. And that has been out of order for the last ten days. Nobody bothers.'

And this e-mail came up for discussion in the morning meeting. 'So, what do we do?' Kalam asked me in his typical style. I said, 'Sir, I shall speak to the Collector.' I did and the job was done. And Kalam gets an e-mail from the girl, 'Uncle, thank you. The see-saw is working now.' But she added, 'But uncle, when can I meet you, you are so good.'

Let me tell you another instance. On 20 July 2006, a certain lady sent a letter to the President complaining that her five-year-old stallion had developed laminitis and that members of the riding fraternity were spreading unsavoury rumours about it. She went into clinical detail about the laminitis that had afflicted her stallion, the meticulous care that she was taking to rid it of the disease, the food that she was feeding him, etc. She concluded the two-page letter typed in single space saying that she would like the President's advice and guidance in the matter. Even this came up for discussion in the morning meeting! And as was appropriate it was consigned to the records after, of course, as Kalam would insist, sending a letter of acknowledgement to the lady.

I have mentioned earlier that Kalam was very keen that all the letters and e-mails that we received were attended to and answered. This had cast a heavy burden on the entire Rashtrapati Bhavan establishment. Even that was fine; what I was worried about was about the possibility of too many references from Rashtrapati Bhavan going out to the officials concerned and making all of them just good enough to be dealt with lightly. I must confess here that my colleagues and I decided therefore to adopt a formula by which only the most important ones would be forwarded to the state governments for a report; others would be just forwarded for information and those still remaining would be just sent saying that they were received at Rashtrapati Bhavan. A large number of recommendations also used to come for admission to various colleges, for professional and other courses; they were forwarded with a specific clause that 'this was received here and is being sent to you with no recommendation and for disposal as per extant rules and procedure'.

We also used to receive hundreds of letters from people recommending others and even themselves for awards ranging from the Padma Shri to Bharat Ratna and for appointment as governors and ambassadors. I note this with shame that even some retired chief secretaries belonging to the 'illustrious' service to which I belonged had also sent their resumés eulogizing themselves and explaining why they were fit to be appointed governors. I had never known that the service had fallen to such a low and it was my duty to inform them accordingly, which I did.

Perhaps Kalam never knew this. I did not tell him either.

✦

'Suppose this fellow does some funny thing?' Kalam wondered with his characteristic concern. It was that day's morning meeting. And the paper that evoked Kalam's comment was a letter addressed to him by a person from a village in Pune district. In that letter, he had dwelt at length on the travails that he and his family were undergoing because of acute financial difficulties. The letter also spoke of various illnesses that he and his wife were suffering from, the need to find suitable employment for his unemployed son, as too an appropriate match for his grown-up daughter and so on. The writer went on to say that he had knocked at the doors of district authorities, MLAs, MPs, ministers and even had written to the Government of India for immediate help but nothing was forthcoming. He was approaching the President as the last resort and if he also did not help him, the only course open to the family was to commit suicide 'en masse'.

The President was moved. He asked me what we could do. The hard-boiled bureaucrat in me made me tell him that such cases would be far too many and that if the President started dealing with such problems, there would be no end to it. This obviously did not satisfy Kalam. He said he was prepared to give the family some money from his personal account so that they did not resort to any extreme step. I advised him not to do that but said that I would write to the Collector to look into the problem and give whatever help that was possible. I would also write to the SP concerned to take adequate precautions to ensure that the family did not precipitate matters, as mentioned in the letter. Kalam agreed, though rather reluctantly.

I proceeded accordingly. Apparently the Collector was able to extend some help to the family, which certainly was a boon to them. That we did not get any further letter from the Pune villager was a positive signal that gave immense satisfaction to Kalam.

However, this incident had a problematic fall-out. Word spread in that village first, then in the district, in the state and finally almost all over the country that if you had any problem, you could write to President Kalam and he would intervene. Kalam's permanent refrain in all his speeches everywhere that anyone could send messages to him on his e-mail ID and that he would get a reply within 24/48 hours made the situation absolutely uncontrollable. His mailbox swelled out of proportion, bursting at the seams, and stretching us to the limit too in the bargain.

I could tolerate even all this, but what I couldn't stand was the impunity with which many approached him. Kalam was soft-hearted to a fault and many started exploiting that quality in him mercilessly. The new strategy adopted by them was to pour out their problems, real or imaginary, and seek immediate intervention by him, failing which they all threatened that they would commit suicide; if necessary, in front of Rashtrapati Bhavan.

Kalam took all these threats seriously and wanted us to

act. He didn't want a single loss of life on account of this. For us it was hell. The last straw was when people started seeking appointment with him, failing which, they said, they would commit suicide. This was nothing but emotional blackmail. Having hit the rock-bottom of my bureaucratic patience which, in any case, was constricted and shallow, I told him one day in one of those morning meetings that that day also I had received a couple of letters in both of which the signatories had *promised* to commit suicide. My sarcasm was not off the mark, but Kalam's wince spoke volumes. I didn't and couldn't say anything further, and went on to discuss other papers which, in my view, were less nonsensical. I finished and left his room, feeling totally small in front of this giant of a man who had risen to such heights by sheer goodness of heart that is so rare in this world. He had made it amply clear to all of us that he was where he was and we where we were only to solve the people's problems and there was no circumventing or short-circuiting that process. He showed it by example, not only while sitting in his office at Rashtrapati Bhavan, but even when he was on tour to various parts of the country.

I remember what happened when he visited Goa. After the visit was over, we got a complaint from there that while making arrangements for the President's visit, the police went overboard trying to clean up the area and in the process evicted hundreds of street vendors who had been earning a livelihood by selling their wares on the roadside.

Not only that, the allegation also was that during the process of eviction, the police even threw away their belongings, including the items that they had spread out on the pavement to sell. We do not know to what extent this allegation had substance. However, on Kalam's express instructions I conveyed his concern to the authorities in Goa telephonically and also that punitive action would be taken against those responsible if such an incident was ever repeated. He also insisted that all help should be given to those affected and I received assurance on all these concerns from the officials in Goa. All this was conveyed to Kalam, giving him some comfort. Kalam was always willing to go all out to help those who genuinely needed assistance.

When the tsunami struck in 2004 and VIPs were busy visiting the affected areas, Kalam readily agreed to our suggestion that he should not visit those areas yet because any such visit would only hamper the rehabilitation work which needed to be launched on a war-footing. The states' resources of men and materials could not be diverted for providing VVIP security. He monitored the rehabilitation and relief measures on a continuous basis from Rashtrapati Bhavan itself. His sincerity and compassion were genuine attributes, not traits that were used to gain public favour.

I think people knew this. No wonder he was called the 'People's President', which he was till his last day in office.

# 12

Ever since Kalam became President, requests had been pouring in from various institutions wanting to shower awards and distinctions on him. Many government institutions and local administration bodies had also sent in requests to name roads, schools, hospitals, libraries and other buildings after him. Kalam's view was that even if they had genuine regard and respect for him as a person, these requests might have more to do with his position. He therefore consistently refused the offers and I would reply to them accordingly.

President Kalam set much store by high values and professional propriety. All of us know only too well that normally when people assume positions of power and authority, they tend to bestow quite a lot more attention on the places they come from. This could be by way of creation of institutions there, or providing facilities, or building a palatial house, or visits that are more frequent than required.

Kalam was an exception here too. He belongs to Rameswaram, in Tamil Nadu, and ever since he assumed charge as President, requests had been pouring in directly to him as also to those like me who were in his secretariat urging him to visit his hometown, lay foundation stones, or use his authority to help get roads repaired or provide new roads and a whole lot of other things. All things that are normally considered 'doable', or rather, for leaders trying to please their constituencies, necessarily to be done. Not so for Kalam. He was the President of the whole of India and that he came from Rameswaram did not entitle it to any special privilege. During his conversations with me, he had made it clear that he would visit Rameswaram not on priority, but only in the normal course—that is, after his visits to areas that needed his attention more. No wonder his first official visit as President of India was to Gujarat in August 2002, which was in the glare of national as also international attention, specially in the first half of 2002. And the first of his only two visits to Rameswaram came full two years later—after he had already visited twenty-five states and three Union Territories. Similarly, I wonder if any VVIP before him had visited the North-East as frequently and thoroughly as Kalam did.

The same policy prevailed in respect of his visits abroad. His first visit abroad came after he had already visited most of India. Once he told me that he would go abroad only after he had visited the entire country, but he had to swerve, though marginally, from his plan, as the foreign visits are planned well in advance, and the first trip came after he had been to twenty-two states and three Union Territories.

He had, however, one regret when he quit office in July 2007—he could not make it to Lakshadweep at all as President. Not because he did not try but because of the weather conditions ruling it out from the security angle whenever he planned a visit there. That regret will remain with him.

Abraham Lincoln once said, 'Honest statesmanship is the wise employment of individual manners for the public good.' That seems to ring true for Kalam.

# 13

That President Kalam chose Gujarat, which was in focus after the riots in February–March 2002, to be the first state to visit officially as head of state did send a few messages across. Or, as they say in newspaper parlance, 'caused a stir in political circles'. I wouldn't say that either the Gujarat government or the Central government was unnerved at this, but certainly they did sit up and take notice of it. But what happened immediately after his return to Delhi from this visit did make waves all over, particularly in the political and legal circles.

On 19 August 2002, a proposal was received in Rashtrapati Bhavan requesting the President to promulgate an ordinance as approved by the Union Cabinet three days earlier, on 16 August.

The Constitution of India vide Article 123 under Chapter III—Legislative Powers of the President—empowers the

President to promulgate ordinances during the recess of Parliament. This Article is specifically meant for enactment of urgent legislation when the Houses of Parliament are not in session. The ordinance so promulgated will have the same effect and force as an Act of Parliament. However such an ordinance would cease to operate at the expiration of six weeks from the re-assembly of Parliament unless before the expiration of that period Parliament dis-approved it.

The ordinance sent to the President in August 2002 related to amending the Representation of the People Act, 1951 so as to amend Forms 2A and 2E appended to the Conduct of Election Rules, 1961. Thereby a sworn affidavit would be filed by the candidates with a view to rationalizing the information required to be furnished by them. Declaration of assets and liabilities by the elected members of legislatures was expected to bring about transparency to the whole process and enhance the credibility of elected representatives. It was also expected to help curb criminalization of politics.

The whole issue of the ordinance arose out of a Supreme Court judgement in a certain civil appeal before it in May 2002.

The President studied the ordinance in great detail with reference to the directions made by the Supreme Court in its judgement. He noted that the proposed ordinance, while incorporating some of the directions of the Supreme Court, remained silent on some others like declaration of assets and liabilities of the contesting candidates and their spouses and dependants and the educational qualifications of the contesting candidates. Pointing out that therefore the provisions of the proposed ordinance were not wholly in consonance with the perspective requirements of the Supreme Court, Kalam returned the proposal to the Cabinet for its reconsideration and advice.

The Cabinet reconsidered the matter and reiterated its proposal, stating however that the proposed Representation of the People (Amendment) Bill, 2002 would take care of the aspects of declaration of assets and liabilities of the spouse and dependants too of the elected candidates. It was pointed out to the President that the ordinance was required precisely because a departure was being made from the directions of the Supreme Court, which formed the basis of the 28 June 2002 order of the Election Commission of India.

The proposed ordinance thus reconsidered and reiterated by the Cabinet was resubmitted to the President by the Prime Minister. It was approved and promulgated by the President on 24 August 2002.

There has been a general feeling that the President of India is just a rubber stamp and that his office is only a ceremonial one. Although some of his predecessors did act on a few occasions to dispel this myth, Kalam's considered and thoughtful action based on the law and facts as mentioned in the preceding paras had a telling effect. Perhaps none expected a scientist such as him with no grounding at all in politics to exercise his constitutional powers as the President of India so effectively and with copybook precision even before he completed thirty days in office. He made it amply clear that any proposal that was put up to him would be subjected by him to the strictest scrutiny and that he was not there to simply sign on the dotted line.

One might now wonder why, then, Kalam chose to sign the ordinance on 24 August 2002. The answer is simple. Kalam wanted to be constitutionally right and proper. The Constitution makes it mandatory for the President to approve a proposal submitted to him by the Cabinet. This stipulation is as per Article 74 of the Constitution of India as amended vide the 42nd Amendment in 1976. However the 44th Amendment of 1978 gave the President one chance to refer back such a proposal for reconsideration, but then, once that proposal is reconsidered and resubmitted in whatever form, he is bound constitutionally to approve it.

As President he had taken the oath to preserve, protect and defend the Constitution. He acted precisely in that spirit.

# 14

I noticed early on that Kalam was mortally afraid of even the slightest slur on the presidency. He was not able to stomach any news report that even remotely criticized Rashtrapati Bhavan. In my view, he had carried it to the extreme. Caesar's wife had to be above suspicion, but even there I thought there was a limit. He didn't.

The President's Bodyguard (PBG) is a cavalry unit—perhaps the oldest remaining in the Indian Army. The horses still behave like horses even when sometimes a few of those riding them behave like you-know-what.

On an unfortunate day, it dawned on one of those mentioned above in the PBG to exceed the bounds. The next day's newspapers carried the news on the front page; forget about Bush and Blair—the Buddha Jayanti Park in New Delhi hogged the headlines. 'Rape in Rashtrapati Bhavan' screamed the Press. Kalam, normally so composed,

The author with President A.P.J. Abdul Kalam.

The President, just after he was sworn in on 25 July 2002.

Kalam bids farewell to K.R. Narayanan, the 11[th] President of India.

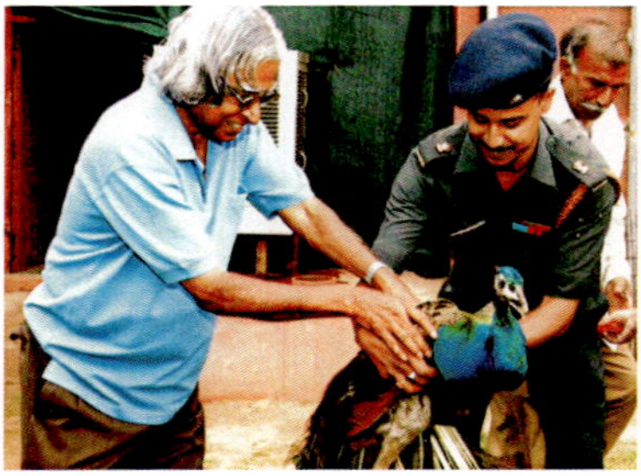

Presidential care for a peacock that had fallen ill and was restored to health.

At the Bio-diversity Park of Rashtrapati Bhavan.

Drumming it up with Sivamani, one of the four artistes who comprise the music group 'Shraddha', in an impromptu performance.

4 March 2006: From one Bharat Ratna to another, Thank You. This was shehnai maestro Bismillah Khan's last public performance.

Explaining his pet project PURA to Gen. Pervez Musharraf, President of Pakistan.

Kalam with U.S. President George Bush and his wife, Laura.

Kalam with Nelson Mandela, a meeting that was very special to him, during his visit to South Africa.

Addressing the European Parliament, the first President of India to do so. (Inset) His speech went well beyond the scheduled twenty-five minutes, but received resounding applause all the same.

Addressing the Jawans at Siachen.

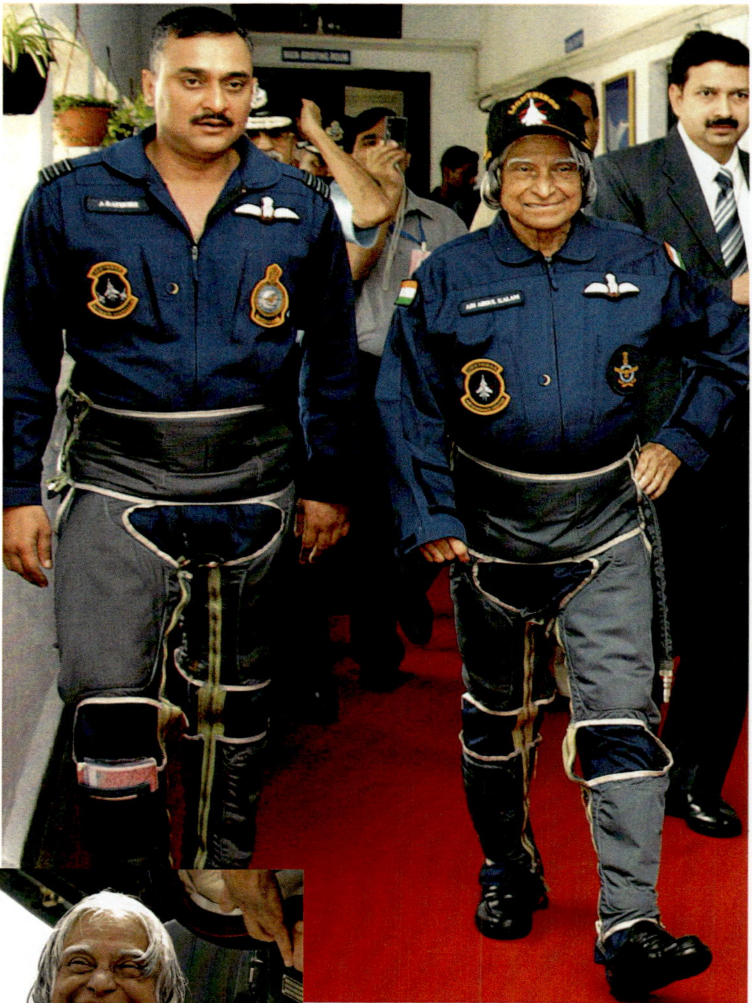

Seventy-plus, but very much in pilot mode: Kalam on his way to the Sukhoi flight, the first time a President flew in a fighter aircraft.

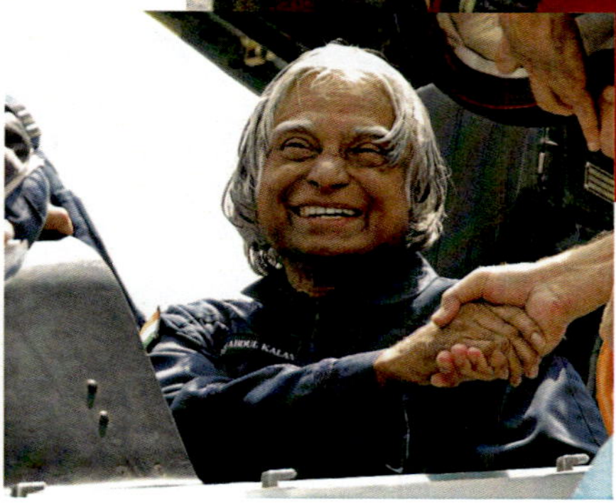

One of his ambitions was to become a fighter pilot. His delight after the flight on an IAF Sukhoi 30 MKI in June 2006 says it all.

was more angry than I had ever seen him, tearing at his hair that in any case was so handy and ringing me up to know what had happened. For once, the voice was not cool at all. He was screaming. I told him I would check and tell him what exactly had happened.

A constable of the PBG, while he was off duty, strayed on his stroll to the Buddha Jayanti Park where he allegedly raped a girl. The Press was quick to trace the culprit's place of posting to Raisina Hill and hence the headlines the next day. The police were doing their job as was the army, and the offender was being dealt with according to the law. I was aghast at the publicity that this incident elicited. I told the President that this was an individual's aberration and that he should not lose his sleep over it, but I knew he would. The Chief of the Army Staff holding forth on the despicable conduct of this member of the PBG, editorials condemning the incident and what have you. All because the person belonged to the Guard deputed to Rashtrapati Bhavan. There was no end to it.

I had a terrible time tackling this issue, but the last straw came a day later. I was in my office. There was a call from a journalist in Chennai. 'Mr Nair, I am . . . from Chennai representing, you know, the very popular journal . . .' I had not heard of that journal at all. Poor me! Yet, my blood pressure rose, the medicines that I had taken in the morning notwithstanding. 'Yes,' I said and waited for him to say what he wanted to say.

'I am talking about that rape. Don't you think you could have stopped it from happening?' he asked. If he had been anywhere nearby, I would very soon have been guilty of assault, at the least. I don't know even now how I kept my temper in check, something I am not known for. I simply said, 'Yes, I could have. If only he had asked for my permission before raping her, I could have denied it. If he had asked for half-day's casual leave saying that he wanted to rape a girl in the Buddha Jayanti Park in the afternoon, I could have rejected it. Unfortunately, he did not ask for my permission at all.' I was not able to complete that sentence. The great journalist rang off and has not spoken to me ever since.

Kalam's ultrasensitiveness was irritating. He knew he was in a glasshouse and stones could be thrown, but then there were limits to what he could do about it. I say this in spite of the fact that I was only too well aware that there were many people waiting with stones. Even then!

# 15

He pressed the bell and the bearer came. 'Please remove this fellow,' he pointed to the empty glass in front of him which had contained cold water a while ago before Kalam made him an 'empty fellow'.

'You know, Mr Nair,' he said, 'even birds and beasts have feelings like all of us. You saw that peacock that could not open its mouth and how it was weeping without crying. Our surgeon is great; he did a miracle and she (Kalam wasn't bothered about the gender) is so happy and is dancing around.'

Kalam was referring to Maj. (Dr) Y. Sudheer Kumar, who successfully removed a tumour that was preventing the peacock from even closing its mouth. It couldn't eat a thing; it was in pain, but Dr Sudheer Kumar cured it of all its aches and pains, removed the tumour and let it dance its way back to its flock.

For Kalam, everything was important. Be it a bee or an animal—all were human beings, 'good fellows'! And he wanted all of them to be good human beings. The invariable question he asked whenever any file went to him for appointing persons in various institutions was, 'Is he a good human being?' And most of the time we had to say 'Yes.' I don't know if we were lying. He trusted us and the files would be cleared. We couldn't afford to have too many vacancies in all those institutions!

# 16

Kalam has an intense side to his personality that many other scientists too display. Leave alone the Rudra Veena, which he was used to playing, art and culture fascinated him as much as rockets and missiles.

Rashtrapati Bhavan, on his initiative, started a series of cultural programmes called Indradhanush. Over fifty-three performances were staged at the Rashtrapati Bhavan in front of an invited audience. Not only the artistes of repute, but those aspiring to join their ranks were encouraged to perform. Ustad Bismillah Khan's last performance was at the Mughal Gardens. Rasika Chaube, my colleague and Internal Financial Adviser, was the architect of the series, under Kalam's guidance. Among the artistes who performed were classical dancers, vocalists, sufi singers and musicians. As an introduction to Indian music and dance for anyone, it was pretty complete.

In November 2006, we had a session under Indradhanush with Shankar Mahadevan, U. Shrinivas, Sivamani and Loy Mendonsa in the open air. The performance drew a large audience and was a smash hit, as expected. But the climax was yet to come. The programme was over, the souvenirs given, the vote of thanks yet to be said. And Kalam walks up to the stage, has a word or two with Sivamani, the drummer, and tries his own hand at the drums, watched by a delighted audience. Now Sivamani presides over an awesome range of instruments—drums, cymbals and other percussion devices—and just to sit in the centre of that array is, to me, an act of daring! Kalam did it with aplomb and, I think, did a fair job for a novice. Certainly the audience enjoyed his impromptu performance, and the beat he came up with.

While eminent artistes performed at Rashtrapati Bhavan, Kalam was very particular about encouraging young and budding artistes too. And it was not only in music and dance but painting and sculpture as well. On every 26 January and 15 August exhibitions were organized where creations by budding artists were displayed at Rashtrapati Bhavan and Kalam made it a point to spend considerable time with all the artists. Needless to say, his patronage so openly exhibited, gave a tremendous boost and inspiration to the young artists to excel.

Nothing prevented Kalam from going out of his way to acknowledge and encourage wherever he saw talent and creativity. During one of his tours to Coimbatore, he happened to meet Krishnamurthy, a renowned vocalist, but unfortunately extremely physically challenged having no limbs—neither arms nor legs. This however did not prevent Krishnamurthy from looking at the brighter side of life. Kalam was impressed by Krishnamurthy and his positive attitude and invited him to Rashtrapati Bhavan for a performance on 18 July 2007. Kalam also ensured that the entire travel-related expenditure of Krishnamurthy and his accompanying artistes was borne by Rashtrapati Bhavan.

# 17

Kalam always kept himself busy with one thing or another—but they all had a bearing on development, part of his mission to generate an atmosphere conducive to making India a Developed Nation by 2020. Hence, whenever he addressed any audience—be it the youth, the farmers, the scientists, the parliamentarians, the judiciary or any other—there was always a message to impart. We are used to having leaders who only are keen on speaking something; but Kalam was one who had always had something to speak—and every time he spoke out.

I recall his address in the Central Hall on 21 March 2005 while presenting awards to outstanding parliamentarians. The President is constitutionally required to address Parliament at the beginning of the first session every year. However, this address, though delivered by the President, is actually that of the government. It is the government's policy statement and the President's personal views and suggestions, however noble they may be, do not normally find place in the speech as it is drafted by the government and approved by the Cabinet. But Kalam had different ideas. The speech delivered to Parliament in 2003 did contain quite a few paragraphs that were included in it on Kalam's specific request. This was basically because of the perfect equation he had with A.B. Vajpayee, the Prime Minister. The subsequent years also saw similar 'inclusions', though to a very limited extent. I had told him that there was no need to feel bad about it because the whole world knew that it was not his speech but that of the government. Kalam must have realized why I was saying so, but he never looked convinced or satisfied.

It was a golden opportunity that presented itself to him when he was invited to present the Outstanding Parliamentarian awards. I advised him that he should not miss this chance; perhaps this was one of the rare opportunities that he would get to speak out his mind to MPs. I reminded him that under Article 79 of the Constitution of India, Parliament consisted of the President and the two Houses, and that therefore he had every right to say whatever he wanted to say to the members because he, like them, was an integral part of Parliament. He was very happy.

In his speech he elaborated on the distinction between politics as we see it normally and developmental politics. He urged the MPs to adopt a positive and constructive approach free of narrow, parochial and selfish considerations and work for the all-round development of the nation. He hit the nail on the head when he plainly spoke of the political parties' 'compulsion for incremental numbers' which led to 'tradability of legislative seats', which in turn facilitated horse-trading. He made an impassioned appeal to dispense with 'political adventurism' and asked the members to engage themselves in a thorough introspection 'to grow up to the expectations that were enshrined so diligently and optimistically by the founding fathers in our Constitution so that India sustained itself and grew as a mature, vibrant, democratic nation'.

The speech was well received, certainly by the public when it was reported in the Press. The President had had his say in Parliament!

There were numerous occasions when he addressed the judiciary. Whenever he did so, he emphasized the need for quicker dispensation of justice. The ever-increasing member of cases pending disposal was a source of constant worry for him. His repeated refrain on this score did move the powers-that-be to initiate action for reducing the pendency, but as it happens with government moves in many other cases, this also, in its pace, let snails overtake it with impunity! Kalam was sad that precious little could be done on this account during his presidency. His disappointment in this regard was not hidden.

Kalam's address in 2007 at the Ramnath Goenka Awards for Excellence in Journalism function was among his best. Emphasizing the need for the media to give a wide berth to sensationalism, he called upon it to play a positive, fearless and proactive role not only in conveying news and information in their proper perspective, but also while doing so, creating an atmosphere in which creative work was made possible for all-round development. According to Kalam, journalism was truth expressed in intelligible language for the information and education of readers. He was so deeply involved in the discussion with the panelists that followed his address that he threw all security and protocol stipulations to the winds. The photograph that appeared in the media the next day said it all. I have included it here.

✦

Just as he spoke, he used to read too.

'Have you seen this?' Kalam asked me one day, showing me a document of over 400 pages which, obviously, was the product of a committee. 'You may like to go through it. There must be something useful in it.' Kalam was optimistic; I was not.

All of us are only too well aware how good we are at constituting committees and commissions on any issue. And how some of these panels when they themselves get tired of wrangling umpteen extensions, dish out reports that serve no real purpose and are consigned to a musty corner after submission. But whenever such reports, which we found tedious and irrelevant, came Kalam's way, he wanted them to be studied and it fell to our lot to go through them and brief him. We couldn't bluff because we knew that even the cursory glance that he must have had through these documents would have given him some idea of what they contained and with the capacity that he had to remember things once seen or read, any such attempt on our part wouldn't work.

We didn't dare not that Kalam would have cross-examined us. He was a leader, but he led in silence—a quality devoutly to be wished.

# 18

The general election of 2004 yielded a mixed result. Kalam, as the President, had an important role to play in the appointment of a new government. In the process, however, he became the target of many who could present conjecture as truth, and weave stories that had nothing to do with fact. As Shakespeare wrote in *King Lear*, 'I am a man more sinned against than sinning', and Kalam would have been justified in saying so too, though he is not one for self-pity.

The results were out but no single party had a majority. The nation waited. I think it was four days later that Kalam called me to ask his favourite question, 'What do we do?'

I had already thought of this and held detailed consultations with Barun Mitra who, though in the IAS, knew the law and the niceties of constitutional law as well as any lawyer. 'Sir,' I said, 'As the President of India, you have to satisfy yourself that there is a party or a coalition of parties who can form a stable government in your view. And then, you have to invite the leader of that party or the coalition of parties to form the government.'

'So, what do I do?' again he asked. 'I cannot continue to wait indefinitely.'

'True, sir, but things are reasonably clear. You have to be personally satisfied that there is possibility of forming a government which will be stable. None has approached you so far staking claims. Yet, going by the reports in the media, print and visual, the Congress with the support of some other parties appears to be in a position to form a stable government. And the same sources say that Smt. Sonia Gandhi has been chosen as the leader. In my view, therefore, you should send a letter to her requesting her to meet you.'

I drafted the letter and he signed it on 17 May 2004—only a letter inviting Sonia Gandhi to Rashtrapati Bhavan the same day.

I further told the President, 'Sir, she will come with letters of support from various parties. You do not have to read all of those. Just leaf through them and ring the bell. I shall be in the ADC's room (which is adjacent to the Study) with the letter to be signed by you, appointing Smt. Sonia Gandhi the Prime Minister of India. Please sign it, shake hands with her and congratulate her. You should also ask when she would like to be sworn in.'

'Okay,' he said. The letter inviting Sonia Gandhi for discussions was dispatched.

We were informed that Sonia Gandhi was meeting the President at 12.15 p.m. on 18 May 2004. I had to do my homework. I prepared a letter from the President appointing her as the Prime Minister.

The appointed hour came. Sonia Gandhi arrived with Dr Manmohan Singh. I waited in the ADC's room, alert for the bell, armed with the letter (yet to be signed) from the President appointing her the Prime Minister of India. Minutes ticked by. The bell rang. I hurried out with the papers—only to see Sonia Gandhi and Dr Singh leaving.

I ran into the Study. There he was and as soon as he saw me, he said, 'Mr Nair, you told me she would come with letters of support, but she came just for discussions. She said she would come again tomorrow with the letters of support from other parties. I said, "Why wait till tomorrow? I am available any time this afternoon or this evening. You please come as soon as you are ready with the papers. My papers are ready for you."'

'Right, sir,' I said. 'We will wait.'

Wait we did. The message came that Sonia Gandhi would meet the President at 8.15 p.m. on 19 May. I was ready again with my draft letter to be signed by the President. Precisely at 8.15 p.m. Sonia Gandhi drove in along with Dr Singh. I waited in the anteroom. The moments ticked by.

The bell rang, and I went in. The President told me that he had been informed that Dr Singh would be the leader of the Party. The letter said he was nominated as the leader of the Congress Parliamentary Party and as the prime ministerial candidate of the party. Letters of support from other parties were also there.

Having been told thus, I went back to change my letter. Now, the President was appointing Dr Manmohan Singh the Prime Minister. Dr Singh stood by in all humility and thanked Sonia Gandhi. The President congratulated the Prime Minister-to-be and I, having done my job, retreated.

I thought it had all ended; no, it was just the beginning. The rumour mills had already started working. They said the President refused to swear in Sonia Gandhi as Prime Minister. Some said Kalam advised her not to stake a claim. Some scribes made Kalam a hero saying he did not blot the nation's pride by appointing her the Prime Minister! How many editorials and 'learned' articles there were by people on what they saw, heard or learnt when none of them was anywhere near. But then, they had the space in print and television in view, and a gullible, captive readership and audience.

The citizenship of Sonia Gandhi was the issue for them. The Supreme Court had already decided on it. Even so, many representations used to come to the President on this subject. For us in Rashtrapati Bhavan, it had already become a non-issue. The Supreme Court's verdict was clear. And the President was fully aware of it.

The President would not lie. He was aghast at what the media wrote. Rashtrapati Bhavan issued a cryptic press release saying that the newspaper reports claiming such a refusal were not true. I told the President that we would not get embroiled in this matter; let the rumours circulate, the truth would still prevail.

It still pains me, however, that even after so many years, this 'puzzle', though it is a puzzle only to those who want to see it as one, remains unresolved. There were any number of occasions when what actually happened at their meeting could have been clarified by those concerned. But none did it. The issue used to come up for conjecture on plenty of occasions, particularly when the possibility of a second term for Kalam was being talked about. Many prompted me to persuade Kalam to speak out about what had actually transpired, but I resisted any such temptation. For I had absolutely no doubt that it did not behove either Kalam's dignity or the dignity of his office to come down to issue clarifications where none were necessary and get involved in irrelevant controversies.

Politics, perhaps, is as much about perceptions as reality.

# 19

23 May 2005, Moscow. As usual cold, but the rooms were warm. I was comfortably ensconced in my room at Hotel Kempinski. 11.15 p.m. Moscow time. The knock at the door beckoned me to the Presidential Suite. I judged it must be something really serious that had to be discussed as Kalam never bothered his officers after office hours or on holidays. Except in emergencies.

I went to the suite. There he was in his blue shirt and the characteristic smile, though the brow was more furrowed than normally.

'I had a call from the PM,' he said. 'He spoke to me for about twenty minutes. This was about dissolution of the assembly in Bihar. The Governor has sent a report about horse-trading going on, and the only way to save democracy is to dissolve the assembly. The Cabinet has considered the Governor's report and the recommendation is coming to me here to dissolve the assembly.'

A little background here. Elections to constitute the new legislative assembly of Bihar were held in February 2005. No party or combination of parties was able to get a majority. The Governor explored all possibilities of government formation and being of the opinion that no party or coalition of parties was able to form a stable government, he recommended the imposition of President's Rule in the state with the assembly being put in suspended animation. The Cabinet in its meeting held on 7 March recommended the same to the President and the proclamation in this regard was signed by the President under Article 356 of the Constitution the same day. The proclamation was also approved by the Lok Sabha on 19 March and by the Rajya Sabha on 21 March.

Subsequently, the Governor in his report dated 21 May 2005 to the President recommended dissolution of the Bihar Legislative Assembly in view of the allurements made by the Janata Dal (United) to the Lok Jan Shakti Party MLAs to form a breakaway faction and join hands with it to cobble up a majority and stake claim to form the government in the state. The Governor was of the view that such undue influencing of the MLAs would distort the verdict of the people and felt that the House under suspended animation should be dissolved to provide the people of the state with a fresh opportunity to exercise their mandate.

The Cabinet in its meeting on 22 May endorsed the

assessment of the Governor and recommended to the President the issue of a presidential order under Article 174(2)(b) of the Constitution for dissolution of the Bihar assembly.

'What do we do?' he asked me.

'Let's see the papers, sir,' I said. We waited in silence, but not for long. The papers came in a few minutes faxed from Delhi. Kalam's private secretary handed them over to me in his presence. They gave the same points that I have mentioned. The Union Cabinet had considered these and endorsed the Governor's decision for dissolution of the assembly. Presidential assent was required.

I went through all the papers. The President had to act on the aid and advice of the Council of Ministers. Thus there were the reports of the Governor, the recommendation of the Council of Ministers and the twenty-minute call by the PM to the President. The material before the President was unassailable. We discussed the issue in all its aspects for more than an hour.

I advised him, 'Sir, please sign.' He signed. I have no regrets, nor should he have any, notwithstanding the criticism from those who were supposed to know the law, who knew it and yet seemed to have forgotten it—some conveniently, some otherwise!

✦

I am none to question the wisdom of the highest court; it is supreme. The learned judges would have their own valid reasons to arrive at the verdict that they passed. The dissolution of the Bihar assembly was held unconstitutional by the Supreme Court, by a majority verdict.

And then all hell broke loose. The Court did not make any remark about the President by name or office; what was judged as unconstitutional was the presidential order. This was enough for journalistic moghuls—I can think of no other term—and lawyers of nonexistent eminence to go on the rampage; the moghuls seeking Kalam's resignation and the lawyers bemoaning the lack of legal and political sagacity on his part. As if, of course, they possessed these in ample measure. People who could not even spell 'constitution' wrote treatises on that document. Poor Kalam. The man from Rameswaram who by sheer dint of personal effort and diligence had rocketed himself to this position was down in the dumps.

The days that followed were grim and the atmosphere in Rashtrapati Bhavan gloomy. The eloquent and voluble Kalam was mostly silent. I could well imagine what he was thinking.

A couple of days followed in this vein. Kalam called me to his room and I entered to see him sans his usual smile and there was nothing 'fantastic' about it. I sat down and he looked me straight in the eye and said, 'Mr Nair, I have decided something.' I knew what he had decided because the hand pointing to his pocket said it all. I leaned forward and said 'Sir,' and I was cut short. 'No, Mr Nair, don't say anything. I have taken a decision according to my conscience.' Hurt and to be honest, angry, I sat back and a heavy silence followed. He didn't say anything more, nor did I, for I was not allowed to. I knew the paper in his pocket was what the journalistic moghuls wanted.

Two days went by. One great thing in India is that there is no dearth of advisers. If there is one post in the Government of India that anyone can occupy even without recommendation, it is that of an Adviser. Deep thought is not an essential requirement—the advice can be proferred without thinking. So Kalam was surrounded by a sizeable clan of that ilk, including one 'Adviser' who gave the Rig Vedic interpretation of the Constitution of India, sending Kalam into a spin that would have been the envy of the rockets and missiles that he had himself made and launched!

Several days passed thus. New experts emerged in the Press, some geniune but many of quite dubious calibre.

He called me again. 'Mr Nair, I want to discuss Bihar.' This time I cut him short, respectfully. I knew I was in front of the President of India. 'Sir,' I said, 'that day when I wanted to say something, you said no and I had to shut up. Now sir, what has happened that is new?' He simply looked at me and I, seeing the distress he had been undergoing, cursed myself for my impatience, though unintended.

'Mr Nair, I could have done two things. I could have

sent back the proposal to the Cabinet for reconsideration. Or at least, I could have waited till the next morning.'

My patience was wearing thin. I knew I would never be given even the Presidential pardon reserved for condemned prisoners for saying this. But I was respectful yet forthright—perhaps two attributes that don't always go together.

'Sir,' I said, 'I am talking to a scientist who is the President of India—not a politician President. A scientist goes by logic and reason and I am going to ask you questions on this and you have to give me answers as a scientist President on that basis.' He didn't expect this from a bureaucrat like me but the scientist in him responded to the idea. I saw the flicker of a smile on his face after many days. He said, 'Yes.'

'Sir, we were in Moscow. What did you have before you? Three reports (I would call them unassailable and well-argued even if I don't hold any brief otherwise for whoever wrote them) from the Governor, the recommendation and advice of the Council of Ministers and the telephonic conversation that the Prime Minister had with you. What other incontrovertible information to the contrary did you have to send back the proposal? If you were in Delhi, I can imagine, any of the known leaders or anybody else could have spoken to you, personally or on telephone. There in Moscow did anyone speak to you? Did you have any information other than the one that was before you? On what grounds would you or could you have sent it back?'

He thought for a while. 'Or, I should have waited till the next morning,' he said.

'Why, sir,' I asked. 'You have been telling us that any proposal that comes to Rashtrapati Bhavan should be dealt with with alacrity and that there should be no delay at all in disposing of it. In this case, what reasons can you give for delaying it till the next day?'

He looked at me, paused and said, 'Mr Nair,' he said, 'I wish you had represented me in the Supreme Court!'

With that, then, I shall rest my case!

# 20

Gen. Pervez Musharraf was visiting India. A visit by the President of Pakistan is always a significant event, and there was the usual hubbub in diplomatic circles, as also in the Press. Among his appointments was a call on President Kalam.

I went to Kalam a day before the visit. 'Sir, General Musharraf is calling on you tomorrow,' I said.

'Yes, I know,' he replied and waited, wondering what I was about to say.

'Certainly, sir, he will raise the Kashmir issue with you. You have to be prepared for the same,' I concluded.

Kalam paused for a moment, looked at me, smiled and said, 'Don't worry, I shall deal with it.' His confidence was reassuring, yet I left his room wondering how he would deal with an issue which could nettle the best diplomats, and had derailed one famous summit meeting, the one at Agra.

Besides being at the heart of several conflicts with that country.

Evening came, after an eventful day in which a cricket match between the Pakistani and Indian teams was the highlight. The General's remark about the hair of star batsman Dhoni added colour to the news reports.

7.30 p.m. General Musharraf arrived in a cavalcade of cars and was led to the North Drawing Room on the first floor of Rashtrapati Bhavan. Kalam received him in state, ushered him to his seat and sat next to him. The Indian and Pakistani officials occupied their appointed places. The call began, slated for thirty minutes.

Smiles on both sides; pleasantries exchanged. And Kalam began. 'Mr President, like India you also have a lot of rural areas and don't you think we should both do whatever is possible to develop them on priority?'

What could General Musharraf say but 'Yes.'

And then Kalam really began. 'Mr President, I will tell you something about PURA very briefly. PURA means Providing Urban Facilities in Rural Areas.' The plasma screen came alive and the description of what PURA was and what it could achieve lasted a 'brief' twenty-six minutes. General Musharraf evinced keen interest and when it was over, smiled and said, 'Thank you, Mr President. India is lucky to have a scientist President like you.' Handshakes followed and adieu.

Scientists can be diplomats too.

# 21

Mid-February 2006. All of India was in a fever. Not chickungunia or dengue or any other. This was bush fever—pardon the pun. The hubbub was about President George Bush visiting India.

There was frantic activity all over. The state visit of the French President had just gone off smoothly. But now the focus was on laying out the red carpet for Bush. Visits by American presidents are few and far between. Perhaps that was a reason. Or the sea change in ties with that country.

I had a call from a very, very important Office of the Government. The call was from a very senior officer in that Office. In his polished, bureaucratic way, he sounded me that perhaps the carpets in the corridors of Rashtrapati Bhavan could be changed. In an equally controlled voice I inquired why. The reply came: 'Bush is coming.' I am a patient of hypertension and when tension hits I have no patience. As I respected the caller I simply said, 'No, obviously not. Whatever is good enough in Rashtrapati Bhavan for other presidents and heads of state should be good enough for the U.S. President too.' He rang off.

I had a similar call from a very senior functionary from the Ministry of External Affairs. He said, 'PM, at your convenience let us jointly inspect the facilities in Rashtrapati Bhavan. You know, President Bush is coming.'

'I know,' I said. 'There is nothing to inspect. This is not the first time a head of state is visiting. Whatever was good last week for that head of state who visited us is good enough for the one who is visiting us next week too.' This senior officer with whom I had a perfect equation and understanding did not say a word further.

The phones did not ring any further either, at least on this matter.

I had heard that when American presidents came in the past, their secret service and policemen had taken over security even at Rashtrapati Bhavan and officials there were subjected to their security and surveillance. There was much written about in the Press generally about the extraordinary measures they took on such visits abroad by their President. All somewhat intimidating. Whatever, but regarding Rashtrapati Bhavan and their role in maintaining security there, this was not acceptable to me. And I told the President about my views the next day. He chuckled in response, and that conveyed his confidence and trust in what I proposed.

I knew he had approved my approach. That was enough for me.

I made it clear to the Intelligence Bureau that as far as Rashtrapati Bhavan was concerned, the security responsibilities would be entirely that of the Indian police and security agencies and none from another country would be allowed, even to supervise. The only concession that was given was to have just one sniper on top of the building, but hidden and unseen by anyone else. And this we agreed to as a one-off. A similar request had not come from anywhere else before.

President Bush came. What a refreshing arrival, warm and friendly, compared to the hype created by the Press, security and others. The ceremonial welcome was gone through to a T, with the President's Bodyguard in impressive attendance.

The banquet in honour of the visiting dignitary was an event in itself. That was the second time a banquet was being held in the Mughal Garden lawns. I do not want to narrate the lengths to which prominent people, including the cream of Delhi society, went for an invite to the banquet. It was embarrassing, to say the least.

The banquet was preceded by the formal call by the U.S. President on Kalam. The plasma screen once again throbbed into life, much to the amusement and astonishment of Bush and his wife, Laura.

The banquet went off very well. At the end of it, Bush

went to the band and congratulated them for their performance.

Bush expressed his appreciation of the welcome in a handwritten letter to President Kalam. The letter is included in the appendices.

Mrs Laura Bush wrote to the President too thanking him for the hospitality. We on our part found them a charming couple.

The tricolour continued to fly atop the Rashtrapati Bhavan proudly.

# 22

'Who took my pencil while I was away?' It was my father, fuming. We were living at Thodupuzha in Kerala, where he was District Munsiff. He had an office table at home and some basic stationery for dealing with case files. Incidentally, there was no other table in our house and no other stationery.

I was in the fifth class. Something in my homework had to be underlined and I took the liberty of using his official pencil for doing so. Then I put it back where I thought it had been resting. I was wrong, and he found out.

None in our house had the courage to say 'No' to him, leave alone telling him a lie. So, I came forward and said, 'I . . . I took it for underlining, Achan . . .' I didn't even have the nerve to say sorry.

'You didn't know that office materials are only for office purposes and not private use?' This was followed by three lashes of the cane (that he always kept close by) on my body.

I was taught a lesson—a lesson that I thought I had learnt and had served me well in life.

I had thought I had seen the ultimate in rectitude. I was wrong. With due respect to my departed father, I found that there was more to learn.

May 2006. 'You know, Mr Nair, my relations are coming for a week or ten days. Please ensure that it is kept totally private and there is nothing official about it.' It was Kalam telling me about the upcoming visit of fifty-two of his relations starting from his elder brother who was ninety years old, right down to a one-and-a-half-year-old great-grand nephew. I knew he meant every word of what he said.

They came; they stayed for eight days. They went to Ajmer Sharif; the younger ones went shopping in Delhi too. And then they left.

Extraordinarily, not once, not even once was an office vehicle used. Specially as it was such a large number of people. Kalam paid rent for the rooms occupied by them in Rashtrapati Bhavan. Even each cup of tea was paid for by him! The bill came to Rs. 3.52 lakh, and was paid by the President from his pocket. He didn't publicize it, but I mention it now because I think people should know. I hope he won't mind my mentioning it. After the Thodupuzha incident where I could not stand in front of my father, here I stand now in respectful salute to this man and what he showed me in his unassuming way.

There are several other examples. Perhaps even better

ones. I will mention one that comes to mind. November 2002. Ramzan time. Fasting, ending in festive Iftaar dinners.

Kalam, a devoutly religious man, asked me, 'Mr Nair, why should we have this Iftaar dinner? In any case, the persons who are invited to these dinners are already well-fed. Why waste money? How much do you spend on this?' I said I would get back to him since it was the first time I was overseeing the Iftaar dinner.

I called the Comptroller of the Household and asked for details. He said the cost would be close to Rs. 2.5 lakh for the dinner.

I informed the President. He thought for some moments. 'Why don't we give this money to orphanages? What do you think?'

'Absolutely fine, sir. God will be grateful to you.' I answered.

'You choose the orphanages,' he told me. 'Please ensure that the money is not wasted,' he added.

He had a glint in the eye. I knew what he meant. I was to ensure that the material was distributed to orphanages on the basis of need and proper utilization without basing the choice on religion or sect.

I organized teams. No money was to be given. Rice, flour, pulses and blankets and sweaters were purchased and the teams went to twenty-eight orphanages and distributed them. The children were pleased. I reported the bare facts to Kalam.

But there was another surprise in store.

He called me again. I was alone with him in the room. He looked around and said, 'You have given all that material with government money. I want to give my own money for Iftaar. I am giving you a cheque for Rs. 1 lakh from my personal account. You use it the way you did with the government money, but don't tell anyone that I gave this money.'

I used the amount in the same judicious way as I used the government money.

I admit I did tell others about his gift from his personal account, though.

The President as a submariner: Aboard the INS *Sindhurakshak* on 13 February 2006. The submarine went down to a depth of 50 metres.

The Supreme Commander with Field Marshal Sam Manekshaw.

Kalam with writer and columnist Khushwant Singh, whom he visited at his home.

Kalam at a breakfast meeting with Members of Parliament from the North-East.

Kalam is a natural teacher, as is evident from this photograph.

Instant rapport: With children of Indian origin on one of his visits abroad.

People wait to offer New Year greetings to Kalam—in the thousands.

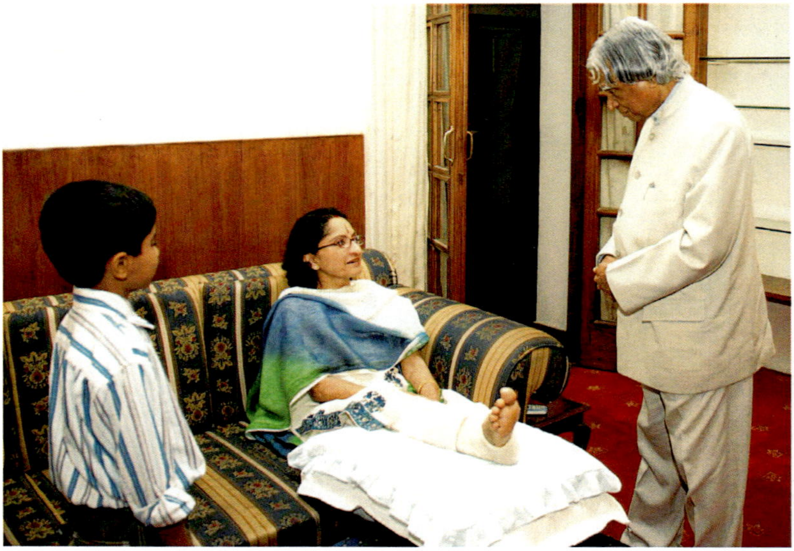

P.M. Nair and his wife could not call on the President as his term was ending. But the President came himself to see the author's wife as she was convalescing after fracturing her ankle.

Kalam with the new President, Pratibha Patil.

The President breaks protocol: Kalam takes the stage at the Ramnath Goenka Journalism Awards ceremony. (*Indian Express photo*)

With the Prime Minister, Dr Manmohan Singh, and his wife, at his farewell on 25 July 2007. Sonia Gandhi is partly visible behind Kalam.

Bidding goodbye at the ceremonial send-off at Rashtrapati Bhavan.

The President clicks his team.

Relaxing with the rudra veena.

# 23

The President's tours abroad. The Presidential plane AI-1 Air-India Special Flight would be full with all enjoying the facilities in style. Kalam would be in his special cabin with a select few who were always around whether he wanted them to be or not, even when mostly it was the latter. I recalled that at the end of an earlier foreign trip, an astute foreign service officer had remarked, 'PM, you have cleansed the Rashtrapati Bhavan premises with insecticides, pesticides and wormicides, but I find the leeches are still on.' This hadn't registered with me then. Now I realized what he meant. How true!

Once the plane took off the airline staff on board went all out to ensure that we were comfortable.

A decent interval and then the inevitable drinks—the full array, be it a Bloody Mary, plain vodka, scotch and soda or a soft drink, fruit juice or chilled water.

Spirits rose, as too volubility. Even PJs got more than their share of laughter. There was always the threat of the President dropping in any moment and the first class passengers kept a place handy to hide their drink whenever he came in.

'Hello, how are you.' The warm greeting that all knew would come and yet wanted to be done with so that the remaining part of the journey and the glasses remained good and bubbly. Kalam had made it a point to have a word or two with everyone, including those from the Press, after which the entourage would be left to enjoy their food and drink. He would be back in his cabin with a couple of his private secretaries and aides to give the final touches to what he would say on arrival. Some of the presidential guests who had no reason to be there, but who were taken along out of sheer presidential courtesy, I have ample reason to believe, used that time to cloud his mind against other members of his team—an attempt that never got off the ground even in repeat tries because Kalam had an uncanny sense of the validity or lack of it of what was being said. In the same way that he is an uncanny judge of people. He couldn't be led by the nose!

The touchdown and the take-off would follow from country to country as scheduled with these interesting episodes in between but then on the return journey to India, the teacher in him would take precedence over everything else and he would ask all to write down in a page or two about what they had felt and experienced on the tour. Even the ministers and MPs who accompanied him were not spared; but none complained or even grumbled. Such was Kalam's persuasive capacity and ability to unite his team for a common purpose.

# 24

President Kalam's trip to Mauritius was one of his memorable visits abroad. It was preceded by a visit to Myanmar, which was significant too as there hasn't been much interaction in recent years with this neighbour.

We landed at Port Louis around 4 p.m. on 11 March 2006. A reception followed, and then, as usual, a crowded schedule of events.

I looked forward to this visit for one particular reason. The Presidential visit proceeded with the normal round of formal calls and visits and banquets. The Mauritians and the Indians there thronged the streets in welcome. I, however, looked for Chung, as I remember his name was—I forget the full name though—Chung who had come from Mauritius to attend a course at Manchester University along with me in June 1978. I looked for him but without success.

One of the high points of the visit came on 13 March.

We were at the lunch hosted by Dr Ahmed Rashid Beebeejaun, the Deputy Prime Minister of Mauritius. Halfway through the lunch, the host stood up and thumped the table for silence. He wanted to make an unscheduled speech. He spoke of the age-old ties between Mauritius and India based on commonality of culture, values, outlook and other aspects. And then he said, 'Your Excellency, the President, Dr Abdul Kalam, you are the son of Avul Pakir Jainulabdeen, you are the brother of Avul Pakir Jainulabdeen Muthu Maracayer, you are the President of India, and we know you are the son of India—but from now on you are the son of Mauritius too.' After a moment's silence there was thunderous applause, lasting minutes. It was an emotional moment, and many eyes were wet. Mine too. Kalam stood up and folded his hands in a namaste as a quiet acknowledgement of the gesture.

There was one more such occasion. Kalam arrived at the University of Mauritius. After meeting the faculty there was an address to the students. After the address, he wanted to interact with the students, as he always did.

There were about 300 students in the hall. Kalam finished his speech and asked for questions. A lull followed and then a boy stood up. 'Mr President,' he said, 'You spoke about Einstein's troubled childhood; how it did not deter him in his path to greatness and glory. But how was yours?'

Kalam smiled, and said, 'You know I also had a somewhat difficult time in my younger days. I had to get up early, around 5 o' clock, go to three schools—I mean madrasas—and then come back, do my homework for the school quickly before going on my bicycle to distribute newspapers. Then I go to school. I come back in the afternoon. Then I take my cycle again to go and collect the money for the newspapers that I distributed in the morning. You know, we had no electricity in our place then. I had to study in the evening. My mother was very nice to me. She would give me kerosene a little more than what she gave others (he showed the extra amount with his thumb and index finger that would have covered an inch and a half!) and I would study late into the night, but remembering that I had to get up early in the morning to go again. Okay?'

There was stunned silence. I looked around. The students were moved. It was an emotional moment, some looked as if they might cry. And there was Kalam, still smiling, waiting for the next question.

# 25

In October 2006, a parliamentary delegation of the European Parliament called on President Kalam. The delegation was led by their President, Joseph Borrel Fontelles. After their discussions with Kalam, President Borrel extended an invitation to him to address the European Parliament.

Kalam accepted the invitation. They wanted his visit preferably in January 2007, but Kalam's tight schedule couldn't accommodate it. Under the rotational presidency, Joseph Borrel was to quit the post by the year-end, but then he had passed on the message to his successor, Hans-Gert Pottering. And the invitation stood.

Kalam's address to the European Parliament comprising twenty-seven nations was fixed for 25 April 2007 and he was allotted twenty-five minutes for the address.

It would be the first time that a President of India would address the European Parliament. It would be a significant occasion, hence we did not want it spoilt by exceeding the time allotted for the speech. I made it a point to tell him day after day, at the risk of being obnoxious, that he should limit his speech to twenty-five minutes. The overrun to the twenty-sixth minute would not exactly bring glory to him or the nation. The Foreign Secretary, Shiv Shankar Menon, told him the same thing. Nalin Surie, Secretary (West) in the external affairs ministry, advised him similarly. Kalam heard them all quietly.

Two days before our departure for the foreign tour, the draft of his speech to the European Parliament came to me. Twenty-nine pages! I stiffened. How could he read out twenty-nine pages in twenty-five minutes? I went to him and reminded him of the time limit and how his speech did not seem to fit the time allotted. 'Okay, okay,' he said. 'I will edit it, don't worry, I will not exceed the time limit.' Thus assured—but still unsure—I came back.

The day of his address arrived. The European Parliament hall in Strasbourg, France. Much bigger than our own Central Hall. The hall was full. Doordarshan was making last-minute adjustments to its equipment for the live telecast of the address. NDTV was also checking its links. We were all in the visitors' gallery, my colleagues and I. A sense of expectancy all around.

President Kalam had the scheduled preliminary meeting with Pottering for about ten minutes and then they entered the hall. There was an introduction of a minute and a half, and then the President began his address. Minutes ticked by. The audience rose to applaud him twice. It was close to twenty-five minutes and there was no sign of his stopping. The Power Point slides kept on coming. I started perspiring.

The allotted time was already over. Half an hour, thirty-five, forty minutes . . . My discomfort was all too evident to anyone who looked at me. Then I heard Kalam say, 'I have composed a poem for you. This is from Mother Earth to the European Parliament. Shall I read it out for you?' he said in his innocuous way. And having received assent, he read it out.

> Beautiful Environment leads
> To beautiful minds
> Beautiful minds generate
> Freshness and creativity.
>
> Created explorers of land and sea
> Created minds that innovate
> Created great scientific minds
> Created everywhere, why?
> Gave birth to many discoveries
> Discovered a continent and unknown lands
> Ventured into unexplored paths
> Created new highways.
>
> In the minds of the best
> Worst was also born.
> Generated seeds of battle and hatred
> Hundreds of years of wars and blood.

Millions of my wonderful children
Lost in the land and sea
Tears flooded many nations
Many engulfed in ocean of sadness.

Then, then came the vision of European Union,
Took the oath,
'Never to turn human knowledge,
Against ourselves or others.'
United in their thinking,
Actions emanated,
To make Europe prosperous and peaceful,
Born, the European Union.

That 'Glad Tidings' captivated
The people of the planet of my galaxy.
Oh! European Union, let your missions
Spread everywhere, like the air we breathe.

He finished and the members stood up again and gave a thunderous ovation. Forty-five minutes had gone by. Kalam said 'God bless you' and sat down. I too relaxed, finally, though still dazed, and so proud of him as an Indian.

President Pottering rose to thank Kalam. 'We have never heard such a speech. Thank you, Mr President' was the gist of it.

The formal lunch followed. It was a lunch in Kalam's honour. Fully vegetarian! Kalam had carried the day.

Later in the day, one to one, I asked Kalam, 'Sir, how

did you choose to exceed the twenty-five minutes given to you? I was worried.' He smiled benignly and said, 'You know what I did. During our introductory meeting, I told their President that you gave me only twenty-five minutes, but I have composed a poem for you and this may take some more time. And he said "Ok, go ahead, you take my time too."'

The incident was reminiscent of a similar situation when Kalam was to attend a meeting of the Pan-African Parliament in Johannesburg in 2005. There was, however, no address scheduled. But Kalam told me, 'You just get me inside the Parliament and leave the rest to me.' And sure enough the Chairman introduced him to the Pan-African Parliament and invited him to address the House. In his address, Kalam laid out his plans to set up the Pan-African e-Network with India's help and expertise. This project, which showcases India's expertise in the field of IT, will provide tele-education, tele-medicine and e-connectivity to all the fifty-three countries of the African continent. And all this because of a short but well-thought-out statement to the Pan-African Parliament!

Kalam's programme in South Africa was as usual jampacked. The high points of the programme were, apart from the address to the Pan-African Parliament, his visit to Pietermaritzburg by a special train that retraces Gandhiji's famous journey.

To recount, it was from Durban station, on 7 June 1893,

that Mahatma Gandhi had embarked on the train journey that would change the course of his life. He boarded the train in order to travel to Pretoria, where he was due to meet with some people in connection with a court case. A first class seat was booked for him. The train reached Pietermaritzburg station at about 9 p.m. A white passenger who entered the compartment was disturbed to see it occupied by a 'person of colour' and returned with two officials, who ordered Gandhiji to move to the van compartment. A constable was called who took Gandhiji by the hand and pushed him out of the train. His luggage was also taken out and the train continued without him. Gandhiji spent the night in the waiting room. It was winter and the weather was bitterly cold. Although his overcoat was in his luggage, which he had left where it was and had been taken charge of by the railway authorities, Gandhiji did not ask for it, fearing further insults. Gandhiji contemplated returning to India but decided that such a course would be cowardice. He vowed to stay and fight apartheid. 'My active non-violence began from that date,' Gandhiji would recall. We had all read all about this.

At Pietermaritzburg station there were four plaques in the waiting area of the railway station. Exactly where Gandhiji was forcibly evicted on the platform is not known. However, on the basis of the length of the train he was travelling in and where the train would have stopped, a granite column has been erected indicating the closest place. The station attracts a large number of visitors and has become a place of pilgrimage. Kalam became one such pilgrim.

Kalam's meeting with Nelson Mandela at his home was another memorable occasion. Mandela was not in the best of health and it was Kalam who helped lead him to where people had gathered to meet them. The photograph included in the book speaks for itself. I consider this one of the most precious moments of Kalam's presidency, for Mandela too stands for the same values and ideals that he holds so dear. I feel fortunate to have been present at their meeting.

# 26

The new Chief Justice of India (CJI) was to be sworn in. Justice Y.S. Sabharwal. The function was being held in Durbar Hall. It was full with more than 500 people. The CJI-to-be sits alone in a chair midway between the audience and the presidential podium. As Secretary to the President, it was my privilege to announce his name after the fanfare and the singing of the National Anthem that marked the beginning of the proceedings.

The guests had arrived; Justice Sabharwal was seated in his special chair and my colleagues and I waited for the fanfare heralding the President's arrival. Since there were a few minutes left, I went to Justice Sabharwal and congratulated him. Thanking me for my greetings, he said Farook had already told him about me. M.O.H. Farook, presently India's Ambassador to Saudi Arabia, and Justice Sabharwal were friends. Farook was Chief Minister of

Pondicherry, now Puducherry, under whom I worked as Chief Secretary to the state government. Justice Sabharwal looked at me and asked, 'So, how is it, working with the President?'

'Great, sir,' I said, 'because I can say no to him.'

Justice Sabharwal looked at me sceptically and waited for more. 'Sir, in these days of only yes sir and nothing else, here is a boss who happens to be the President of India who can take a no to what he says. Only I have to tell him logically and reasonably why. That is the scientist in him and for my no's I give reasons in adequate measure. He has a patient pair of ears and a very sharp brain that he never flaunts.'

The fanfare sounded, and the rest of the ceremonies, followed by the inevitable tea. After the function I came back to my room and contrary to my normal routine, sat back reflecting on our conversation. That led me to reflect on an incident that had happened a few days earlier.

Kalam used to consult legal pundits on issues that bothered him or where the advice given to him by us needed to be buttressed by legal precedent.

During his presidency, a fair number of mercy petitions from those sentenced to death whose appeals had been turned down by the Supreme Court had come in, to add to the similar petitions left over by his predecessor. Kalam had always maintained that he wouldn't like to give an order to take away a life since he was in no position to give a life. I used to violently oppose this view. I had asked him how he could forgive, for example, one who had killed in cold blood seventeen persons of a family including three children four to six years old. He used to say that God was up there to punish them. Such persons, whom we call criminals, should be reformed to become 'good human beings'. Our arguments led us nowhere. He left his 'legacy' too—mercy petitions awaiting a decision—to his successor, in good measure.

In the meanwhile, he had consultations on the issue of capital punishment with legal luminaries including former chief justices of India. I remember one such occasion. Kalam was sitting with one such famous legal personality discussing the whys and why-nots of capital punishment. I was in the adjacent room since I had been told that I might be called. And fifteen minutes into their conversation, the bell rang and the ADC came to me saying 'Sir, you are wanted there.'

I went in. The President and his guest were on a sofa and I sat down opposite them. The guest said, 'Mr Nair, we were discussing capital punishment. His Excellency has really clear views on it and you know them. I agree with them. What do you say?'

I looked at the President. Kalam knew what I was going to say. He smiled. 'Shall I speak out, sir?' I asked. He nodded. And I spoke out respectfully, but in complete disagreement. The legal luminary was taken aback. The conversation ended and I escorted the guest out.

His car drew into North Court and the door was opened.

He looked at me and said, 'This is the way you speak to the President of India?'

'Yes, sir,' I said. 'That is his strength and that is my strength too.'

He got in and the car sped off.

There can be freedom of speech even for a bureaucrat!

# 27

Kalam became President at the age of seventy. But the years sat lightly on him. His indomitable spirit, intense determination and tenacity of purpose infused in him the youthful vigour that many far younger would find difficult to match.

I remember his engagements in one of his trips to Kerala. After the third programme was over, the Governor told me, 'Mr Nair, I am going home; I cannot keep pace with him.' Kalam had fifteen—fifteen!—more programmes to go that day. And he did complete all of them, only to prepare himself for a tougher schedule for the next day.

He had many firsts as President. His visit to Siachen, the highest battlefield in the world, a hostile and icy area where temperatures drop far below zero and the altitude can make breathing difficult, his submarine adventure at Visakhapatnam aboard the INS *Sindhurakshak* S63 and then the flight in the supersonic SU-30 aircraft are some. I was in my office watching on television as he prepared for the flight, and felt quite nervous. Perhaps unnecessarily, as one of his early ambitions had been to become a pilot.

The flight took place on 8 June 2006. It was a forty-minute sortie during which the plane climbed to a height of 7.5 km, flying at supersonic speed. Kalam piloted the aircraft for approximately fifteen minutes. As he stepped out of the plane at Air Force Station Lohegaon, near Pune, he expressed his happiness in having his longstanding dream of flying a fighter aircraft fulfilled. 'I am a contented man. My childhood dream has been fulfilled,' he said. He was briefed earlier on the sortie profile and cockpit layout to familiarize him with the various switches that he was required to operate in the air. The sortie included mild manoeuvres, simulated air-to-air attack and air-to-ground strikes.

On 2 April 2004 Kalam made the historic visit to Siachen glacier. As usual, it was a busy schedule. On arrival at the base camp situated at a height of about 18,000 ft, he addressed the officers and jawans, praising the commendable job they were doing in defending the country. He also warned about the dangers to the fragile ecology of the glacier. To state the obvious, it was remarkable that he went up to this height at all, as one needs to acclimatize oneself to the rarefied air.

The President is Supreme Commander of the armed forces. It was only befitting then that he gained some first-hand knowledge of the environment in which they operate.

✦

A.P.J. Abdul Kalam had many firsts to his credit, even as the President of India. His domestic tours numbered 163 and foreign visits 7. More than the number, extraordinary by itself, was the intensity of the tours.

His visits to the states in the North-East speak for themselves. Unfortunately the North-East, in spite of DONER (Department of Development of North-Eastern Region) and other initiatives remains neglected. An officer doesn't get posted there from Delhi. He is shunted there. When I was comfortably enjoying my work in the Ministry of Defence as Additional Secretary, I was posted as Chief Secretary to the Government of Arunachal Pradesh. I went and was called a fool by all in the service for doing so. I may not have possessed the wisdom that they did, but I was not foolish enough to say 'no' to that posting.

I had advised Kalam that he should visit the North-East as often as he could. He did more. He insisted on going to the interiors and the villages and wanted to see development works going on. He did not confine himself to the capitals and the Raj Bhawans. This was a departure from the usual VIP visits for the people there.

# 28

This chapter is all about the Office of Profit Bill. Oops, I should say, as it turned out to be a slippery issue to tackle. Many commented on the entire episode as avoidable. Let them have their view; I have my own.

A stray complaint and a decision thereon, regarding disqualifying Jaya Bachchan, a sitting Member of Parliament, for holding an office of profit and thereby incurring the adverse qualification envisaged by the Constitution in Article 102 opened the floodgates. In no time there was a spate of complaints against sitting MPs. The President, as ordained under Article 103, sent them to the Election Commission of India for its opinion. He was bound to act strictly according to the opinion when it was received. No discretion.

Parliament, which is supreme, realized the gravity of the situation. It enacted a law that would nullify the charges of disqualification levelled against over fifty MPs. This law had retrospective effect too. Many expressed concern that the law was enacted in disquieting hurry in the Parliament of the world's largest democracy and sent to the President for assent. I shall keep my counsel since I am not competent to comment on the rights and wrongs of the proceedings in Parliament.

The President's position is very clear in the Constitution. Article 111 gives three options to him: give assent, withhold assent or return the Bill to the Houses with a message for reconsideration—the latter two applicable only in the case of non-money bills. The Article which gives such a *right* to the President also vests the Parliament with a *right* to resubmit that Bill after reconsideration to the President with or without amendments. When that happens, he 'shall not withhold assent therefrom'. The phrasing of the Article takes into account the need to do so without delay.

Exercising this right, the President decided to send a message to Parliament. This was the first time a President was exercising this constitutional right and correctly so. In my view, he would have been at fault if he did not do so. He showed that he was not a rubber-stamp President. The message ran thus:

> I received on 25 May, 2006, the Parliament (Prevention of Disqualification) Amendment Bill, 2006, duly passed by both Houses of Parliament for my assent under Article 111 of the Constitution of India.

2. While having the highest regard for the sagacity and mature wisdom of my fellow Parliamentarians and with due deference to the Parliament, I would like the Parliament to re-consider the proposed Bill:

(a) in the context of the settled interpretation of the expression 'Office of Profit' in Article 102 of the Constitution, and
(b) the underlying Constitutional principles therein.

3. While re-considering, among other things, the following may be specifically addressed:

(i) evolution of generic and comprehensive criteria which are just, fair and reasonable and can be applied across all States and Union Territories in a clear and transparent manner,
(ii) the implication of including for exemption the names of offices the holding of which is alleged to disqualify a member and in relation to which petitions for disqualification are already under process by the competent authority, and
(iii) soundness and propriety of law in making the applicability of the amendment retrospectively.

4. As provided under Article 111 of the Constitution, I, therefore, hereby return the Bill to the Houses for reconsideration with this message.

—(signed) A.P.J. Abdul Kalam
30 May 2006

Those who knew the Constitution did explain it to the nation in ample measure. Some of those who knew it chose not to clarify the issue, and there were others who didn't know very much but chose to wax eloquent and philosophize on what the country, the Parliament and the President ought to do. As in all such issues.

The President had a website where he publicized on every possible occasion his activities and messages to the youth and others. It was easily accessible and people could put queries and he would answer them in twenty-four hours! The site became a conduit for people to offer gratuitous advice and suggestions ranging from withholding assent to the Bill, rejecting it, sitting on it, dismissing Parliament and even resigning rather than assenting to the Bill. Even some cartoonists pontificated on the constitutional niceties of the issue in a way that was no less ghastly than their own cartoons.

Parliament reconsidered the Bill and as thought fit by them, passed it again without any amendment. Of course, the government with due respect to the President resolved to refer the matter to a Parliamentary Committee to evolve norms in this regard. It was perfectly constitutional to do so in both these cases. The Bill was reconsidered and repassed in the meanwhile. The Bill thus repassed came back to the President for assent on 1 August 2006. Having exercised his right under Article 111 of the Constitution, he was duty-bound to discharge his constitutional responsibility under the same Article by assenting to it.

Instead, he kept it with him for many days—in my humble view, too many days. I reminded him of his responsibility orally and in writing. He said he was going by his conscience. I told him that the Constitution of India was the conscience of the President and that the Parliament had also gone strictly by the Constitution. They had not committed any constitutional irregularity. People might have different views about the law. That is a different matter. The judiciary may have its own legalistic view, that is a different matter too; but the President had to discharge his constitutional responsibility. That mattered.

Finally, the Constitution prevailed over conscience. The President assented to the Bill on 18 August—seventeen days after he received it back. I have not been able to stomach this delay even now. Would you fault me if I said that Kalam erred in this? I wish he hadn't courted this controversy, whatever his reason for doing so.

# 29

A lot has been written about Afzal Guru's mercy petition; how President Kalam deliberately kept it pending. It is shocking that this perception was allowed to persist by interested quarters and uninformed columnists.

The facts are thus:

Mohammad Afzal, also known as Afzal Guru, was convicted of conspiracy in the December 2001 attack on the Parliament and was sentenced to death by the Supreme Court in 2004. The sentence was to be carried out on 20 October 2006. The sentence was stayed.

The attack was alleged to have been conducted jointly by the Laskhar-e-Toiba (LET) and the Jaish-e-Mohammad (JEM) groups operating out of Pakistan. Seven members of the security forces, including a female constable, were killed, as were another five still not fully identified men who carried out the attack.

When a person is sentenced to death, a sentence upheld by the apex court, he would normally be hanged unless he is given presidential clemency. For this, the condemned prisoner or his kith and kin or legal representative has to send a mercy petition to the President. The President sends it to the Ministry of Home Affairs, which sends it back to him with appropriate recommendations. The President does not act on his own on such petitions.

Afzal Guru's mercy petition was received by the President on 3 October 2006 and sent to the Ministry of Home Affairs the same day. Till 25 July 2007, Kalam's last day in office, no recommendation had come from the ministry. The President cannot act without that recommendation. That is the freedom given to him by the Constitution as amended from time to time. Then why blame him? Rashtrapati Bhavan did not issue any press release on this wishing to stay out of unnecessary controversy. There is no ambiguity regarding the President's ability to act in the matter.

# 30

Kalam had no pretensions as President. Actually he wouldn't know how to go about it either.

A simple instance. The President has an official photograph, with his signature in one corner, that is displayed conspicuously in all government offices, Indian embassies and important venues including airports. When Kalam became President, he was told about this. The initial demurs from him were dismissed and the blue shirt gave way to a bandgala. Three or four options for the official photograph were produced and Kalam asked me to choose one. I did so and it is the photograph you have seen everywhere, the one with the half-smile and the not-yet-buttoned-up jacket.

'What a shame!' remarked a member of the cavalier service. I asked what was. 'Look at that photo. He is the President of India and the pen that sticks out from his pocket is a Pilot ballpoint pen instead of a Mont Blanc or a Parker!'

I was taken aback but realized there was no point in telling him that India was not guided or identified by Mont Blancs or Parkers. We had learnt to pilot ourselves over sixty years ago—fifty-five years to be exact when this happened.

Kalam was totally oblivious to all this. Perhaps even now. For him, any pen or a pencil was a 'fellow' and he was only keen that that 'fellow' worked. And he had many such 'fellows' that didn't have high brand value but did the job very well, perhaps better than the Mont Blancs and Parkers.

That Kalam was not bothered about the niceties of protocol and cared even less for pompousness was quite evident in the way he conducted himself everywhere—be it at Rashtrapati Bhavan or outside it, including his state visits abroad. We who were among his staff at Rashtrapati Bhavan and more than us, the officers of the Ministry of External Affairs had a terrible time trying to persuade the President to adhere to certain imperatives of protocol, particularly during his foreign trips.

The simplest example of his down-to-earth approach and total absence of any insistence on formalities was evident in his discomfiture when people addressed him as 'Your Excellency'. He knew that perhaps he couldn't avoid being so addressed during ceremonial functions but on more than one occasion, I heard him tell his visitors to avoid using this honorific during day-to-day conversation, official and otherwise. Even so, they did not always accede to his request.

I have a special reason to record it here. In the course of my service pre-Rashtrapati Bhavan days and also as Secretary to Kalam, I had the opportunity to serve under or interact with many governors and lt. governors. Although none of them forced me to address him as 'Your Excellency' during my calls, I had learnt from the officers of Raj Bhavans and Raj Niwases that many of them had been insisting on their being always addressed as 'Your Excellency' and referred to only as 'His Excellency'. My worst experience was when I had to go to a particular Raj Bhavan to finalize the details of the President's impending visit to that state. I was staying at the Raj Bhavan and in the evening I thought I would take a stroll in the sprawling grounds of that mansion. As I was setting out, I was respectfully stopped by an official of the Raj Bhavan. 'Sir, not now, because Madam Governor is out there taking a walk.' I was amazed. The Governor, I knew, was a gentleman, and I had met him only a few hours earlier. I was not aware that there was another Governor in that state, this one a lady. Hence I asked the official who the lady Governor was. He looked amused at my ignorance. With an air of smug superiority he educated me that it was none other than 'Her Excellency', the wife of the Governor. Seeing me bewildered, he explained further that His Excellency had specifically ordered that his 'lady wife' should be addressed as 'Madam Excellency' and always referred to either as 'Madam Governor' or 'Her Excellency' only. This reminded me of one Lt. Governor of a Union Territory who had given written instructions that he should not only be addressed as 'Your Excellency' at all times, but that all files sent to him must necessarily be marked 'H.E. LG'. Well, if a Lt. Governor could insist on files being marked to him as 'H.E. LG', one could go a step further and adjust to 'Madam Governor' too. Thus enlightened, I withdrew to my room.

Since Kalam was a bachelor, there was no scope for 'Madam President' or 'Her Excellency' in Rashtrapati Bhavan in his time. He must certainly have felt relieved to that extent, protocol-wise!

# 31

Kalam's simplicity is well known. It is also genuine. The following instances will bear ample testimony to that.

It was September 2002. My mother had come to stay with me at Delhi. She is a full ten years older than Kalam.

One day, having heard from various quarters about Kalam's personality, and that he always respected age and shunned all ostentation, my mother expressed a desire to see him. Having seen life from a bureaucratic perspective for over thirty-five years, I was on my guard. I didn't want to hurt my mother's feelings; yet I avoided a direct answer in the affirmative and said, 'I shall try'—the bureaucratic equivalent of 'I shall look into it.' I did try, though with considerable trepidation. After all, I was going to speak to the President of India.

'My mother is with me, sir, she wants to call on you at your convenience. I shall be grateful, sir, if you could kindly give a date and time.'

'Fantastic! This Sunday around 12 noon?' came the answer. 'Yes, sir,' and I retreated and hurried back to my house and told my mother, 'Amma, we shall go to the President this Sunday at noon.' Amma was happy and I felt relief and a sense of fulfilment.

Sunday came. My mother accompanied by my wife and I went to Rashtrapati Bhavan. At the North Court, three ADCs were waiting to receive us. We were taken to the first floor in the lift. As the lift doors opened, the ADCs told me, 'Sir, we have been asked to go down and wait.' The ADCs left and there was Kalam waiting to receive my mother. Clad in a shirt and veshti sans all trappings of presidency, he took us to the main drawing room. He sat by my mother's side, I keeping a respectful distance and my wife sitting opposite me. My mother speaks English reasonably well, but she had been rather hard of hearing. She blessed Kalam as an elder sister would her brother and he responded to the blessing in the same spirit.

The meeting lasted about twenty-five minutes and I said, 'Sir, thank you very much; we should leave now.' We all stood up. He said, 'Wait,' and disappeared into the adjoining room, only to return with a beautiful shawl which he presented to my mother. Of course, my mother thanked him profusely and blessed him again. We were moving towards the lift. And then the President asked me, 'Mr Nair, shall I come down to see her off?' The bureaucrat in me came to the forefront. 'No, sir. We shall go. You shouldn't come down.' The bell rang; the lift came and we stepped in. As the doors closed, we saw Kalam standing there, hands folded in namaste to my mother. On our way back home, my mother told me in the car, 'There are lessons to be learnt from him. Learn them.'

Well, I have tried to do so but am not sure if I have succeeded.

✦

Once the President called a former Chief Justice of India, Justice M.N. Venkatachaliah, from Bangalore for a consultation. They were together in the Study for a few minutes, sitting side by side on a sofa. I was called in at the end of this meeting and took Justice Venkatachaliah to his room. We sat in silence for a while, and then he said, 'Mr Nair, this was an experience of a lifetime. I was sitting so close to Dr Kalam and I could feel sensations of godliness and divinity reverberating within me. I was nervous. He is really God's own man.'

It was something I had begun to feel at times myself, but I did not say anything.

Kalam's meeting with Field Marshal Sam Manekshaw was his own idea. The hero of the 1971 war with Pakistan was not in good health, and Kalam decided during his visit to Ootacamund—Ooty—in February 2007 to call on him. Kalam was quick to realize that it is one thing to decorate deserving people with a high title, but quite another to ensure that certain perks and facilities consistent with such high rank are also bestowed on them. Immediately on his return, he set in motion the process to do something meaningful in this regard, and the result was the evolution of a package of benefits to such personalities consistent with the high ranks to which they were elevated. Marshal of the Air Force is the rank in the Air Force equivalent to the rank of Field Marshal in the Army. Sam Manekshaw and Arjan Singh (the first and so far the only Marshal of the Indian Air Force) were to become entitled to this package. That such benefits should be extended to them with effect from the date that they had assumed these ranks was insisted upon and ensured by Kalam entirely on his own initiative.

His call on writer Khushwant Singh was also at his own initiative. They are two contrasting personalities, but the affection and ease that were evident at their meeting showed how well Kalam could interact with diverse people. At its core is a concern for people that explains why the nation wanted him as President again.

# 32

These may be the closing chapters of this book, but ever since Kalam took over as the President of India, new chapters of Presidency were being written almost every day. Perhaps it all started with his having breakfast meetings with groups of MPs, discussing issues of regional, national and even international importance. Though many enjoyed the meetings and found them useful, some were disparaging about them. I even overheard a conversation between two of the participants (one of whom went on to reach a high position where, however, he earned a rather dubious reputation) referring to these breakfast meetings as a tamasha where they detested the class-room atmosphere, the only palatable thing being the fare served later.

Kalam is a born teacher. This was evident from day one when he made it a point to administer oaths of honesty, righteousness, probity and propriety to his audience, mostly of the younger generation, although here again, I heard murmurs of derision. His lectures, which included the occasional poem, extolled the virtues that would make one a good human being.

Kalam assumed presidency fully realizing that his term was for five years. Although he was aware of the fact that nothing in the Constitution prevented a second or third term, he never tried for it even indirectly. But as time passed he became the symbol of the people's aspirations and a role model for the younger generation, and pressure started building up on him to stand for a second term. He didn't give in. As far back as in 2005, he told the audience at a function at Coimbatore that he was waiting for the end of July 2007 to go back to teaching at Anna University in Chennai.

This suited some people very well. It supported their argument he shouldn't be given a second term. After all, he had already decided what he would be doing after July 2007. Politicians dream of gaining the kind of popularity he had. Still has, in fact. One minister rang me up one day and said, 'What is this? The popularity that this man is getting should have come to us. After all, we are the elected people.'

I told Kalam, 'Sir, for God's sake, don't pour cold water on people's aspirations. You have whetted their appetite; you have given them hope. In your words, they see their future, India's future. You can't back out from your responsibility.' He listened patiently. I went on, 'Sir, another thing. Those who don't want you will use your own statement against you. They will say that they respected you so much that when you said you wanted to go back to teaching, which is your first love, they felt they would be doing a disservice to you by requesting you to stand for a second term. That they only want to respect your wishes.'

He did not respond.

In December 2006, a group of statesmen—an endangered species in politics—met Kalam trying to persuade him to stand for a second term. I was not present there, but I have it on authority that Kalam, when they insisted, only told them, 'If all of you want me, I shall not say no.'

As the end of his term approached, people started voicing their views through SMSes and e-mails. Newspapers and TV channels did surveys that showed Kalam's popularity at 80 to 95 per cent, while that of other leaders was mostly in single digits, or just about managed to reach double digits.

Someone remarked that India's President was not elected through SMS or e-mail. True enough. But the people's choice seemed clear enough, even if the politicians took time to work out their choice. Somehow I felt that things had just fallen apart and the Centre could not hold. We at Rashtrapati Bhavan refused to be provoked by the questions of varied kind that were put to us.

There was much hullabaloo about one political combine of parties, the Third Front, proposing Kalam's name. His answer was just as it had been before. There was no question of his contesting and losing. He used the word 'certainty' and far too much was made of it. The less said, the better, because more than enough was said.

India got a new President, a woman—for the first time. She conducted herself with dignity all through the process of nomination and election. She deserves all our congratulations and best wishes.

The reception to the new President and the farewell to the old were moving occasions. The dignity that is called for on such an occasion was fully maintained in all respects.

Yet, one felt a tear or two drop when Kalam waved goodbye as he left for his new home accompanied by the incoming President.

# 33

I had mentioned earlier about the extensive tours undertaken by Kalam throughout the country. Most of the states invited him during such tours to address their legislatures, and he gladly accepted. But none of them was a normal, run-of-the mill address. The entire Rashtrapati Bhavan would be put into overdrive to find out the core competence of each state, the progress achieved and what each state should aim for in the future. Kalam himself would spend hours and days researching and preparing himself for such addresses. By the end of the effort, Kalam had enough material to prescribe developmental missions for each state, based on irrefutable data. And, of course, his suggestions carried the stamp of his vision. Many states like Kerala set up committees to pursue the goals envisioned in the missions. One only hopes they are taken to their logical conclusion. They would be of immense benefit.

Kalam's faith in the youth and his rapport with them have become legendary. He knew that they were the future of the nation and that moulding them properly was the only way the nation would move forward. Not a day passed when he did not find an hour or two to spend with youngsters, hundreds of them, telling them how the future of the nation depended on their honesty, purposefulness and single-minded devotion to achieve the 'mission'—another favourite word—before them. It is unbelievable how he fired their imagination and galvanized them into such a powerful force. He had made it a point to administer a multi-point oath to the youth whenever he had occasion to address them. Catch them young and infuse in them the vigour required to achieve the mission of a Developed India seems to have been his intention.

I must mention here that whatever Kalam did was done in an informal way. He never ordered, but we all obeyed. And it produced results. What better way to accomplish things.

Kalam was extremely proud of the various facets of Rashtrapati Bhavan which he wanted the world to know. This resulted in publication of books like *Mansion Nonpareil*, *The Roses of Mughal Garden*, *Trees of Rashtrapati Bhavan*, among others. Satish Mathur, Director (Administration) and Brahma Singh, OSD (Horticulture) can claim credit for these achievements. Satish Mathur had already been busy with revamping the administrative set-up (which he did remarkably well), yet he could find time to bring out *Mansion Nonpareil*. Similarly, Brahma Singh was primarily responsible for ensuring that the Mughal Gardens bloomed in full glory for all to see and enjoy.

# 34

I should feel guilty if I did not write this chapter.

It was July 2007. All of us were getting ready to leave. I had told the President that I would be vacating my official residence a day before he demitted office—the day I was to relinquish my office too. But God had willed otherwise. On 14 July, my wife fractured her ankle. She had to undergo a major operation and I had to postpone vacating the house by almost three weeks. But Christy Fernandez, my successor, and his wife were very understanding and told us not to worry, there was no need to hurry. Let me thank them for their fine gesture.

We left on 19 August. We had wanted to call on President Kalam before he demitted office; my wife's accident prevented us from doing so. But a surprise was in store.

On 24 July, Kalam himself came to our house to see my wife who was practically immobile at that time, and spent more than fifteen minutes with us. This when he himself had a packed schedule.

We were all so overwhelmed that we could not even say 'Thank you, sir'.

## Thank You, Sir

*Sir,*

*The legacy that you leave behind will be hard to erase. You remain etched in people's memory, and your positive influence will continue to spur them to greater heights because you have ignited their minds.*

*For me personally, these have been a fantastic five years during which I observed, learnt and accomplished much more than I ever did before. And, I hope, became a much better person.*

*For all this and more—*
*Thank you, sir*

*25 July 2007*

# Appendix A

*The following is the edited text of a letter I wrote, which was printed and included photographs, to the staff of Rashtrapati Bhavan towards the end of A.P.J. Abdul Kalam's term as President. It is a thank-you note, but provides a useful summary of some of the improvements that were initiated from 2002 to 2007.*

*—Author*

It was the morning of 14 July 2003. 8.40 a.m. The RAX in my office rang. It was the President at the other end. 'Mr. Nair,' the President said, 'Last night I could not sleep because my bedroom was leaking . . .' I froze. Any other President, and my head would have rolled, though for no fault of mine. Obviously sensing my acute embarrassment, the President continued, as only he could, 'Don't worry. I know you will immediately set things right in my bedroom, but I am worried about those houses in the President's

Estate where they may not have a second bedroom to shift to when the only one that is available leaks.' I hurriedly mumbled a 'Sorry, sir, I shall act just now.'

I sent for my CPWD colleagues and told them about the leaking ceiling. They were equally unhappy such a thing should occur. We then decided on a crash programme of maintenance of all civil installations in a timebound manner. There was no point in rueing that the maintenance of the various buildings of Rashtrapati Bhavan and the President's Estate had not been attended to for decades. I must thank my teammates that the work of maintenance that we took up was completed most satisfactorily and well in time. I am aware of the sleepless nights spent by my colleagues in the public works and electricity departments of Rashtrapati Bhavan in ensuring this. I was also happy to note that none of my colleagues gave me any excuses for the lapse that had occurred. Almost thirty years ago, in Pondicherry, the Raj Niwas was leaking and when I, as Secretary, PWD, posed this issue to a Senior Engineer of the department, the reply that I got was 'No, sir, it leaks only when it rains'!

Friends, I cannot thank you enough for your farsightedness in visualizing the need for and executing a complete revamping of the residential quarters most of which had, with passage of time, become beyond economical repairs. It is a tribute to your abilities that the new buildings that have been constructed are a pleasure to look at and a privilege to stay in. At least for once, the Central Public

Old quarters

New quarters

Works Department will not be accused of being stereotyped and prosaic.

I shudder at what would have happened if our engineers and others had not detected in early 2003 the extremely poor condition of the South and North Courts which were on the verge of crumbling when any vehicle passed over them. The work involved in rectifying the defects was a mammoth affair and I thank our engineers for their fine work.

The entire Rashtrapati Bhavan building has been under thorough repairs and maintenance for the last couple of years. The photographs [some of which are included in this appendix] would show what it was earlier like and how it is now. Even the 'chajjas' have undergone thorough maintenance and those who come after us will, I am sure, thank you all for making this such a wonderful place.

We in Rashtrapati Bhavan are inheritors of a great heritage. Priceless paintings, statues and figurines are scattered throughout this magnificent mansion. Any damage to them owing to lack of maintenance or neglect would be unpardonable. Here again I express my gratitude to my team members for pointing out the deteriorating condition of the priceless paintings in Ashoka Hall, so that restoration work could be commissioned on an emergency footing and the paintings restored to their original glory.

The Children's Museum that was set up in 2003 has been a novel addition to the variety of facilities available in

The splendid Ashoka Hall after the restoration work.

Rashtrapati Bhavan. Both educative and entertaining, this museum has been attracting not only children but also adults, who take great pleasure in finding out how much they would weigh on other planets and are quite pleased when they find they weigh much less there than they do on planet earth! A substantial number of portraits and paintings have been contributed to this museum by children from all strata of society.

The total area of the President's Estate including the Rashtrapati Bhavan per se comes to 329.73 acres, of which the bhavan alone occupies 5.32 acres, Forecourt 18.45 acres and Mughal Gardens 10.47 acres. Rashtrapati Bhavan and President's Estate have a good network of roads connecting the sprawling complex. You all pointed to the need for re-laying the roads, to lay special pedestrian walkways as also build bus shelters. It is a matter of great satisfaction that all these could be done without disturbing the beauty of the verdant surroundings.

Rashtrapati Bhavan has always been known for the Mughal Gardens. These gardens have been enriched and variety added by the dedicated efforts put in by all levels of staff in the garden and PWD. The new Herbal Garden, the Cactus Garden, the garden for the visually challenged are all shining examples of your initiative. The Musical Fountain that was commissioned in 2006 has been a tremendous attraction for visitors. It was noticed five years ago that

The musical fountain

although the President's Estate was heavily wooded, quite a few of the trees had been tampered with and had become hollow, so that they could be conveniently picked up once they fell and their wood utilized. Such malpractices were stopped altogether. Moreover, with a view to undoing the deforestation that had already taken place, a massive tree planting campaign was launched and the results are there for everyone to see. The garden staff deserve full praise for this achievement.

The Bio-diversity Park has been an added attraction to those visiting Rashtrapati Bhavan. Deer, ducks, hares, peacocks among other creatures live in this park and the veterinary staff have been taking care to ensure their well-being.

With a view to enlightening the public on the extraordinary variety of birds to be found in the Rashtrapati Bhavan complex, a special survey was done and a compendium prepared.

The Rashtrapati Bhavan boasts of lakhs of books in the library, many of them very old and priceless. An attempt was made to digitize them and the process is still on. We are sure the process will be carried on and completed very soon.

Sports facilities have been augmented and updated. The golf course, the tennis courts—clay and artificial—the renovated squash court, all of international standards, the football ground, etc. bear eloquent testimony to the interest that you have all shown in sports and games. The icing on the cake came in the form of the Health Centre and the Fitness Centre equipped with state-of-the-art equipment and the guidance of qualified experts available there for all the residents. Table tennis and billiards are an added attraction there. The well-maintained swimming pool rounds off the sports facilities.

Innumerable are the e-mails received at Rashtrapati Bhavan every day ranging from people asking for repair of see-saws in parks to construction and widening of roads to provision of electricity to issues of great national and international importance. Receiving them is one thing and responding to each one of them positively is another. I would like to thank each one of you for the personal interest taken in redressing the grievances expressed through these e-mails. Nothing has been considered unimportant. No wonder people have started looking up to Rashtrapati Bhavan as the 'People's Bhavan'. This would not have been possible but for the dedicated and sincere efforts put in by all of you and allow me to thank you wholeheartedly for that. We are absolutely sure that this tradition will be maintained for all time to come.

I am personally aware of the tremendous responsibilities shouldered by the security personnel and the reception staff of Rashtrapati Bhavan ever since Dr Kalam took over on 25 July 2002. A very large number of people from all walks of life have been meeting him almost every day and clearing them security-wise, looking after them as our honoured guests by seating them properly, giving refreshments and escorting them back after their meeting the Rashtrapati had been, needless to say, a very onerous responsibility. The reception, which is the first destination for every visitor, needed a complete revamp, as my colleagues suggested. In fact, what was being used as a reception was a small room which could hardly accommodate five to seven people comfortably. I would like to thank my colleagues for identifying a place and making a spacious, warm and hi-tech reception room where visitors can now get their passes issued online, take a virtual tour of Rashtrapati Bhavan and have a hot cup of tea as they wait. And these security personnel and the reception staff do their job admirably also on days like the New Year, Diwali and other festivals when thousands of people with families throng the Rashtrapati Bhavan lawns to greet the President. On 1 January 2007, more than 6,000 people met the President and greeted him on the New Year and it took more than four and a half hours for the President to meet each one of them and greet them too. Likewise more than 2,665 farmers from all parts of the country came to Rashtrapati Bhavan to meet the President. I distinctly recall the odds the security personnel had to face in ensuring that this meeting and interaction went through smoothly without a single incident. On occasions like Republic Day, the President had been meeting special groups like policemen, postmen, writers, sportsmen and others separately and these had cast extra responsibilities on our reception and the security set-up. The President's insistence on each one of them being looked after personally added to this responsibility. Medical facilities were also made available on call on such occasions.

My colleagues in the CPWD identified that funds were the major constraint in maintaining the PBG (Presidents' Bodyguard) area which was, as a convention, being funded by the Army. With the joint effort at every level, things have been streamlined and with a regular flow of funds from Defence, the PBG area has undergone a major facelift and is now at par with all other areas of the estate. All because of you, again.

It was because of the overwhelming response and support from my colleagues, staff and their families that we began to hold exhibitions of paintings and sculptures every 15th August and 26th January, thereby encouraging upcoming artistes. But for your support, events like these could not have been initiated and held regularly and successfully.

An area in the basement which was cluttered up and not very optimally utilized has, with your efforts, been turned into a beautiful 'kitchen museum', which is another feather in the cap of Rashtrapati Bhavan. It is also with your joint effort that we are going to open a painting gallery shortly which will be inaugurated by the President around 19 July 2007.

The Mughal Gardens are opened to the public in the early months of every year, and the President specially instructed that we make adequate arrangements to ensure that there was no untoward incident and that all the visitors were looked after very well. Consequently the administration commissioned mobile squads who would patrol the entire area throughout the day providing assistance where required and ensuring that no volatile situations arose. Medical facilities and provision of drinking water at very many points were also ensured for the welfare of the visitors. My thanks to all my teammates, particularly the security personnel, the reception staff, the medical staff and those colleagues who worked ceaselessly on the grounds.

Your interests were not confined to work, sports and games, but covered art and culture too in a very big way. This was evident in the rich cultural programmes held in our Art Theatre and even Mughal Gardens under the umbrella of 'Indra Dhanush'. Not only did noted and acknowledged luminaries in the field of fine arts grace the occasion, adequate opportunities were given to upcoming talent also in these. This would not have been possible but for the patronage extended by all of you. A magnificent manifestation of such patronage is there for all of us to see—the new auditorium which seats 300 people and whose design blends so well with the rest of Rashtrapati Bhavan.

The short time in which this has been made possible and the minute attention given to details regarding the beauty and the technical efficiency of the structure, acoustically and otherwise, is an eloquent testimony to the quality of your work.

The new auditorium

It was essentially because of the tremendous enthusiasm all of you showed that it was possible to organize a Sports and Cultural Festival for all the people in the President's Estate in November-December 2006. It was spread over more than two months and covered a wide array of events, and the residents of President's Estate participated in the festival with unparalleled gusto and enthusiasm without worrying about hierarchy. This was the first time in the history of Rashtrapati Bhavan that such a festival was organized and allow me to thank you all for making it such a grand success. Imagine the President of India spending close to four hours on the final day of the festival and that was indicative of the tremendous success of the endeavour! We are sure that such tremendous success in the pioneer venture will pave the way for this to become an annual feature and all of you will be the beneficiaries for that.

The five years that have gone by have seen a veritable electronic revolution in Rashtrapati Bhavan. Accessing the first citizen through e-mails that ran into a few hundreds almost every day became a way of life with people all over the country. Giant strides were made in the introduction of e-governance and to top it all, a state-of-the-art multimedia studio was commissioned in the bhavan from which the President addressed many a foreign audience in far-off countries. All this was possible only because of your unstinted cooperation and purposeful, dedicated pursuit of the goal of efficient functioning of the office of the first citizen of India.

I have absolutely no doubt that with many of you continuing to be here, the days to come will see still further progress and much more efficient functioning and Rashtrapati Bhavan will continue to maintain its enviable appellation as the 'People's Bhavan'.

# Appendix B

*Below is the text of President George Bush's note to President A.P.J. Abdul Kalam. It was written by hand, rather than typed, as was usual with most such letters of appreciation following a visit.*

3/3/06

THE WHITE HOUSE
WASHINGTON

Dear Mr. President,

Laura and I enjoyed our time with you a lot. The dinner was fantastic, and your briefing on energy was most interesting. Thank you for your hospitality.

You are a wise man with a great heart. We appreciate your leadership, and your care for the education of Indian children.

With very warm regards,

George Bush